Christof Kehr

Einstieg deutsch

German right from the start

Englische Bearbeitung von Sue Bollans

Max Hueber Verlag

Quellen:
Fotos: Aleksandra Križaj, Sauerthal
Seite 31   Fotos (1. und 3.): Bundesbildstelle, Bonn
Seite 13   Karte: Leo58, München

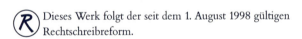 Dieses Werk folgt der seit dem 1. August 1998 gültigen
Rechtschreibreform.

4.	3.	2.		Die letzten Ziffern bezeichnen Zahl
2005	04	03	02	01	und Jahr des Druckes.

Alle Drucke dieser Auflage können, da unverändert,
nebeneinander benutzt werden.
1. Auflage
© 1998 Max Hueber Verlag, D-85737 Ismaning
Umschlaggestaltung: Parzhuber & Partner, München
Layout und Satz: Leo58, München
Druck und Bindung: Ludwig Auer, Donauwörth
Printed in Germany
ISBN 3-19-021609-6

Contents

You have probably bought this book because you are interested in Germany and the German language, and are looking for a first introduction to the country and its people. The 20 units will tell you something about life in Germany, and you will take your first steps in learning the language. People say German is not particularly easy, but you will soon see that it is not that difficult. After all, there are five million foreigners living in Germany, and most of them have learned it. So don't worry, German really can be learned.

When you have worked through this book with the cassette or CD, you will be able to get along in the language, and not just in Germany: German is also spoken in Austria, a large part of Switzerland, and northern Italy. You will learn around 400 words and phrases, be able to ask simple questions and understand most of the answers, as well as hold simple conversations. You will, however, probably not be in a position to have a sophisticated discussion about economic crises, the loss of values, or historical aspects of church music. For this of course you need years of experience with the language and a large vocabulary. But you will hopefully have fun with the new language. You will find that a great deal can be said with only a few words. And you will perhaps even say, *Wunderbar, das war ein Einstieg, ich werde auf alle Fälle weitermachen* (= Wonderful, that was a good start, I shall certainly carry on). More than this we are not aiming to achieve.

We hope this is what you will feel. After all, what brings people together more than a common language?

In the morning in the underground on the way to work, at home when there's nothing worth watching on television, in the doctor's waiting-room, or when you are sitting in the car waiting for your partner to come out of the office, have a look at the book or listen to the CD or cassette ...

How to use this course

This course contains 20 units. It covers the following areas, with four lessons devoted to each: greeting and getting acquainted, shopping, getting around, eating and drinking, and finally conversation. All the units have the same structure to make it easy for you to find your way around:

Devise a learning ritual for yourself. For example, start a new unit at the same time every other day:
- read the text on page 1
- listen and read the vocabulary three times
- listen to the dialogues three times
- learn the vocabulary, and finally
- do the exercises.
If that's enough for the time being, leave the second part of the unit and do it the next day.

■ On the first page a text in English explains what the unit is about, and what people do in Germany.

■ The second page presents the new words with a translation (as they occur in a conversation) followed by a dialogue. Listen to the words and dialogues on CD/cassette several times, learn the meanings and just join in with the speakers whenever you feel like it.

■ The third page consists of a variety of exercises to help you practise what you've learnt: vocabulary exercises, exercises on points of grammar and – most important of all – exercises in communication. Some of these exercises involve listening to the CD/cassette, in other words they help you improve your listening skills. There's a key, by the way, to all the exercises in the appendix.

■ The second part of the unit again begins with new words and a dialogue, and is followed by the

■ second part of the exercises.

■ At the end of every unit there is a text telling you more about the Germans and life in Germany.

Things you'll also find in this book:

This book is designed as a self-study course, but is equally suitable for teaching beginners in a class situation. If you're working on your own, the comments that a teacher might make at a particular point are given in the margin: extra information, amusing notes, or dry explanations of grammatical points – this too is all part of learning a language.

■ After every four units there's a Test based on what you've covered in the preceding block of units. So you can check for yourself whether you have gone over everything thoroughly enough. The correct answers are again given in the key.

■ In addition to the answers for all the exercises and the tests, the Key also contains comments, explanations and comparisons which you'll find useful while doing the exercises.

■ The Grammar summary is a review of the most important grammatical structures that have been dealt with in the book. This is where, for example, you can look up how to conjugate verbs or form the plural of nouns.

- The Dictionary is an alphabetical list of all the words in the book with their English translations and some important linguistic details: with nouns the definite article and plural form is given, with verbs the past participle.

The recordings

Learning a foreign language is not just a question of reading. Equally important are listening and speaking. The CDs/cassettes are there for you to listen to what there is to learn and to practise speaking it. The best way to proceed is as follows:

- Listen to the new words in the A section of a unit with your book open. Note the pronunciation and memorize the meaning of the individual words. You won't have memorized them all after the first listening, so listen again, two or three times. Then shut the book and listen to the words again without reading the translations. In fact there's enough time after each word on the CD/cassette for you to repeat it out loud and thus practise producing the right sounds.

- The dialogue in the A section contains all the words you've practised in context. Try to understand as much as you can, just talk along with the speakers and pay attention to their intonation. That's very important, and anyone can learn it. It can't harm to exaggerate a bit at the beginning.

- One of the exercises in section A is always recorded. Put the book aside when you do this exercise. Listen to the example, then you have a go. The chime signal tells you when it's your turn to speak. You'll hear the correct solution after the speaking pause.

- Follow the same procedure for section B.

All wordlists, dialogues and exercises that are on the CDs are marked in the book with the symbol

The two numbers show which CD and which track the section is on. If you're using cassettes, it might be worthwhile making a list of counter numbers so that you can find the sections you want more easily.

International words

Bank Computer
Hamburger Hotel
Nation Pizza
Politik Radio
Tourist Doktor
Musik Telefon
Demokratie Information
These words are rather
familiar, aren't they?

Magic word

Entschuldigung (= Excuse
me) is always the right
thing to say when you
address someone. It's pronounced *end-shooldy-
goong.*

Mr Nelson Muller, an American engineer, is visiting Germany for the first time. His plane lands at Frankfurt Airport after a six-hour flight. Mr Muller doesn't know quite where to go to collect his case and so simply follows the other passengers off his plane. The route takes him along sterile modern walk ways, then across a busy concourse with elegant shops. Finally he arrives at customs and presents his passport. The official leafs through the passport, looks at the photo, looks at Mr Muller, looks at the photo again and says, *Sind Sie Nelson Muller?* (= Are you Nelson Muller?) *Ja, das bin ich,* answers our friend (= Yes, that's me), and passes through. Ten minutes later, carrying his case, he enters the large arrivals area where people are waiting for the passengers. A lady approaches him and asks, *Entschuldigung, Herr Muller? Ich bin Frau Krug. Willkommen in Deutschland.* (= Excuse me, are you Mr Muller? I'm Ms Krug. Welcome to Germany.)

Entschuldigung.	Excuse me.
Ja, bitte?	Yes (please)?
sind Sie	are you
Herr	Mr
das bin ich	that's me
ich bin	I am
Frau	Ms, Mrs, Miss
Guten Tag.	Hello.

Learning tip

First listen to the words a few times on the cassette/CD. Pay attention to the pronunciation and stress of each word. Then read the words in the book out loud and memorize their meaning.

In German when someone addresses you, you say *ja, bitte?* (= yes please). In English this sounds a little strange …

Entschuldigung.	Excuse me.
Ja, bitte?	Yes?
Sind Sie Herr Muller?	Are you Mr Muller?
Ja. Das bin ich.	Yes, that's me.
Ich bin Frau Krug.	I am Ms Krug.
Aha. Guten Tag, Frau Krug.	Oh. Hello, Ms Krug.

Pronunciation – nothing to worry about!

We don't want to distract you unnecessarily with transcriptions of the pronunciation such as *end-shooldy-goong, sint see frow crook?* Memorize the pronunciation with the help of the cassette/CD, and the spelling with the help of the book. All the new words are on the cassette/CD.

You can also start these dialogues by listening to the cassette/CD. They tell you what to say when you first address someone.

1. Fill in the gaps

If you can't think of the word, then just look at the first dialogue on page 9.

1. Yes? - Ja *bitte* ?
2. Yes, that's me. - Ja, das _ _ _ ich.
3. I am Ms Krug.- Ich _ _ _ Frau Krug.
4. Are you Mr Muller? - Sind _ _ _ Herr Muller?

2. Find the right answer

Only one of the two alternatives makes sense!

Guten Tag.

Some people, especially when they are in a good mood, have a very complicated way of saying hello using lots of words: *einen wunderschönen guten Tag!* (= I wish you a wonderfully good day!). Perhaps this will cheer someone up who hasn't slept well and has woken up in a bad mood.

1. Herr Muller?
   a ■ Aha.
   b ■ Ja, das bin ich.
2. Sind Sie Frau Krug?
   a ■ Ja, ich bin Herr Schroeder.
   b ■ Ja, das bin ich.
3. Sind Sie Herr Schroeder?
   a ■ Entschuldigung.
   b ■ Ja.
4. Entschuldigung?
   a ■ Ja, bitte?
   b ■ Guten Tag.

3. Sort into matching pairs

Simply find the right translation.

1. ja, bitte?
2. Entschuldigung
3. das bin ich
4. aha

a ■ that's me
b ■ oh
c ■ excuse me
d ■ yes?

4. Make a sentence from these words

Here the words have been jumbled up: see if you can sort them out into the right order.

1. bin - das - ich - ja   *Ja, das bin ich.*
2. Seitz?- Herr - Sie - sind   _____
3. Frau - bin - Krug - ich   _____
4. bin - Schroeder?- ich - Thomas _____

5. What international words can you make?

Look for syllables that fit together to make a word. If you get stuck, you'll find some of the words in the margin at the beginning of the lesson.

bur - com - dio - fon - ger - ham - le - mu - piz - pu - ra - sik - te - ter - za
1. *computer*   2. _____   3. _____
4. _____   5. _____   6. _____

wie	what
Sie heißen	your name is
mein Name ist	my name is
aus	from
nein	no
Woher kommen Sie?	Where are you from?
und	and
ich komme	I come
ich heiße	my name is

Guten Tag.	Hello.
Guten Tag.	Hello.
Wie heißen Sie?	What is your name?
Mein Name ist Carlos Saura.	My name is Carlos Saura.
Sind Sie aus Spanien?	Are you from Spain?
Nein, aus Mexiko.	No, from Mexico.

Entschuldigung.	Excuse me.
Ja, bitte?	Yes?
Wie heißen Sie?	What is your name?
Ich heiße Detlef Barber.	My name is Detlef Barber.
Detlef Barber?	Detlef Barber?
Ja. Und Sie?	Yes, and you?
Ich heiße Rita Müller-Proll.	My name is Rita Müller-Proll.

Woher kommen Sie?	Where are you from?
Ich komme aus Hamburg?	I'm from Hamburg.
Aus Bamberg?	From Bamberg?
Nein, aus H-a-m-b-u-r-g.	No, from H-a-m-b-u-r-g.
Aha.	Oh.
Und Sie?	And you?
Ich komme aus Berlin.	I come from Berlin.

Did you notice?

ich heiße = mein Name ist
Both expressions mean the same thing. You can always use either one.

Learning tip

1. First listen to the words a few times,
2. then repeat them,
3. then learn them. It's also helpful
4. to write the words down.

Here you learn how to ask someone's name and say where you're from.

Du or Sie

There are two ways of addressing other people: with children, friends and relatives the *Du* form is used with the person's Christian name or "Granny", "Uncle" etc:
Guten Tag, Oma • Hallo Uschi • Hi Max
Young people, even when they don't know one another, use the *Du* form.
With strangers, colleagues, officials – in fact anyone else who is only remotely connected with you and in particular older people – the *Sie* form is used with the person's surname: *Tag, Herr Brillmayr • Wiedersehen Frau Jacobi*
In this book you will only be learning the *Sie* form. This is all you need at the beginning and everyone will understand.

Miniconjugation

ich komme	I come
Sie kommen	you come
ich heiße	my name is
Sie heißen	your name is
ich bin	I am
Sie sind	you are

You can also simply say
Ich bin aus Berlin.

1. Translate into English

If you don't know, simply look them up in the dictionary at the back of this book.

1. Deutschland *Germany*
2. Amerika _____
3. Mexiko _____
4. Japan _____
5. Italien _____

6. Israel _____
7. Syrien _____
8. Australien _____
9. Österreich _____

2. Find the right answer

As before, only one answer is possible. If your answer is wrong, then look in the key where you'll find out why some answers are wrong.

1. Woher kommen Sie?
   a ■ Deutschland.
   b ■ Aus Amerika.

2. Sind Sie Herr Barber?
   a ■ Ja, das bin ich.
   b ■ Und Sie?

3. Wie heißen Sie?
   a ■ Ich komme aus Deutschland.
   b ■ Mein Name ist Schröder.

4. Sind Sie aus Italien?
   a ■ Ja, aus Hamburg?
   b ■ Nein, aus Deutschland.

3. Sort into matching pairs

The idea is to find the right translation.

1. woher
2. mein Name ist
3. und Sie
4. ich komme aus
5. nein

a ■ I come from
b ■ no
c ■ where from
d ■ my name is
e ■ and you

4. What's your name?

This speaking exercise will help you get used to German names. Some of these may sound familiar.

Ich heiße Hans Schröder.
1. Hans Schröder
2. Detlef Barber
3. Steffi Graf
4. Helmut Kohl
5. Michael Schumacher
6. Johann Wolfgang von Goethe
7. Nina Hagen
8. Egon Krause
9. Wolfgang Amadeus Mozart

5. Where are you from?

Here is a speaking exercise to help you learn the names of a few foreign countries. This is always useful especially if you travel, when you always meet people from other countries.

Ich komme aus Amerika.
1. Amerika
2. Deutschland
3. Australien
4. Italien
5. Israel
6. Österreich
7. Mexiko
8. Japan
9. Syrien

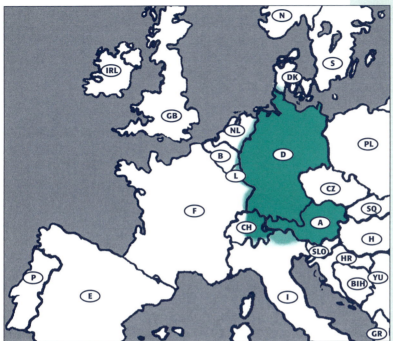

Area where German speakers are to be found

What do northern Italy, southern Denmark, eastern Belgium and southern Poland have in common? In all of them German is spoken. German is the second most important Germanic language, and like English, Dutch and the Scandinavian languages it has developed from a common Proto-Germanic language.

German is regarded as a language with a rich vocabulary and one that is far from simple to learn: there are many small endings to be mastered before you can speak or write with some degree of accuracy. At the beginning, it is important just to chat away, to communicate without worrying about small mistakes. Making yourself understood and understanding as much as possible are, after all, what it's all about.

Since reunification in 1989 Germany has become much more important, but it is only in the countries of Eastern Europe that the German language has become more widespread. Although it is spoken in many countries of the world, it is still not a world language on the scale, for example, of English. Nevertheless, in Brussels, the headquarters of the EU, a Dane and a Greek may well, for example, be found communicating in German.

German-speakers around the world:

82,000,000	Germany
7,900,000	Austria
4,350,000	Switzerland
1,500,000	France
1,500,000	Brazil
1,500,000	Kazakhstan (CIS)
560,000	Canada
500,000	Poland
400,000	Argentina
385,000	Romania
250,000	South Tirol (Italy)
200,000	Hungary
200,000	USA
135,000	Australia
130,000	Czech Republic/Slovakia
110,000	Belgium

German is of course spoken in many other countries too; these are just the ones with the most German speakers.

Greeting:

Guten Tag – is appropriate all day until the evening.
Grüß Gott – is what people say in South Germany.
Hallo – is less formal.

Saying goodbye:

Auf Wiedersehen – is always right, from morning to night.
Tschüs – is what's said amongst people who know one another a bit better: amongst friends and acquaintances.

Ms Krug and Mr Muller know each other now. After meeting him at the airport and taking him to his hotel, she picks him up again the next morning. *Guten Morgen,* she says (= Good morning), and puts out her right hand. Mr Muller shakes her hand and also says *Guten Morgen.* In Germany people usually shake hands when they greet each other. Only relatives and good friends give one another a kiss on the cheek; this is frequent between women, less frequent between men and women, and rare between men. Ms Krug now asks the obligatory question: *Wie geht es Ihnen?* (= How are you?) When the person you ask this answers positively, you start talking about something else. If the answer sounds as if something is not quite right, as you would anywhere, you probe further and ask what the matter is.

Hallo	hello
wie geht es Ihnen?	how are you?
gut	fine
danke	thank you
alles in Ordnung	everything's okay
sehr gut	very well
wunderbar	wonderful
das Leben	life
so schön	so nice, great

If you like something very much, *sehr schön* (= great) is what to say.
Don't get *wunderbar* and "wonderbra" mixed up.

Hallo, Herr Muller.	Hello Mr Muller.
Tag, Frau Krug.	Hi, Ms Krug.
Wie geht es Ihnen?	How are you?
Gut, danke.	Fine, thank you.
Ja?	Yes?
Ja, alles in Ordnung.	Yes, everything's okay.
Ja?	Yes?
Ja, es geht sehr gut!	Yes, I'm very well!
Aha.	Ah.
Wunderbar.	Wonderful.
Aaah.	Ahh.
Ja, das Leben ist so schön.	Yes, life is great.

Ms Krug doesn't seem to believe that Mr Muller is all right. His last sentence is pretty convincing though, isn't it?

Tag is what the lazy ones say.

The full expression is *Guten Tag*. But *Tag* doesn't sound so formal.
Es geht sehr gut literally means "It goes very good."

Find the little word without which the sentence makes no sense.

1. Fill in the gaps

1. Woher _ _ _ _ _ _ Sie?
2. Mein _ _ _ _ ist Kinkel.
3. Wie _ _ _ _ es Ihnen?
4. Das Leben ist so _ _ _ _ _ .

Look carefully to see which of the answers fits.

2. Find the right answer

1. Wie geht es Ihnen?
   a ■ Danke, wunderbar.
   b ■ Danke, aus Berlin.
2. Sind Sie Frau Schumacher?
   a ■ Alles in Ordnung, Frau Schumacher.
   b ■ Ja, das bin ich.
3. Wie geht es Ihnen?
   a ■ Wunderbar!
   b ■ Woher kommen Sie?
4. Heißen Sie Müller?
   a ■ Ja, ich heiße Becker.
   b ■ Nein, mein Name ist Becker.

The simplest of all translation exercises. Don't worry, there are harder ones to come.

3. Sort into matching pairs

1. das Leben
2. Entschuldigung
3. wunderbar
4. so schön

a ■ excuse me
b ■ great
c ■ life
d ■ wonderful

In English of course the "thank you" always comes after your state of health. Notice that Germans say "thank you" even if the answer's "not very well".

4. How are you?

Wie geht es Ihnen? - Danke, gut.

1. gut
2. nicht so gut
3. sehr gut
4. wunderbar
5. alles in Ordnung

guten Morgen	good morning
krank	ill
wirklich	really
nicht	not
vielleicht	maybe
ein bisschen	a bit
kein Problem	it's not a problem, no problem
schlimm	bad

Guten Morgen, Herr Muller.	Good morning Mr Muller.
Guten Morgen.	Good morning.
Wie geht es Ihnen?	How are you?
Nicht so gut, Frau Krug.	Not so good, Ms Krug.
Sind Sie krank?	Are you ill?
Nein.	No.
Wirklich nicht?	Really not?
Vielleicht ein bisschen.	Maybe a bit.
Ohh...	Ohh...
Kein Problem.	It's not a problem.
Nein?	No?
Es ist nicht so schlimm.	It's not so bad.

Maybe Mr Muller is ill, has got stomach-ache, hasn't slept a wink all night and hasn't had breakfast yet. But he doesn't want to say too much to Ms Krug.

1. Sort into matching pairs

This exercise is for your passive vocabulary, to help you improve your understanding.

1. vielleicht
2. wirklich
3. ein bisschen
4. wunderbar
5. nicht so schlimm

a ■ not so bad
b ■ wonderful
c ■ a bit
d ■ really
e ■ maybe

2. Find the right answer

1. Wie geht es Ihnen?
   a ■ Danke, aus Deutschland.
   b ■ Danke, sehr gut.
2. Sind Sie krank?
   a ■ Ja, wunderbar.
   b ■ Ja, vielleicht.
3. Geht es nicht so gut?
   a ■ Kein Problem.
   b ■ Ja, ich heiße so.
4. Guten Morgen.
   a ■ Kein Problem.
   b ■ Hallo.

3. Translate into English

This exercise is for the active vocabulary you need in order to say something yourself.

1. wunderbar *wonderful*
2. nicht so gut _____
3. kein Problem _____
4. das Leben _____
5. wirklich _____
6. vielleicht ein bisschen _____
7. alles in Ordnung? _____
8. so schön _____

4. How are you?

You can answer this question with a short (gut) or a long answer (danke, es geht gut).

*Wie geht es Ihnen?- Danke, es geht **gut**.*
1. gut
2. wunderbar
3. sehr gut
4. nicht so gut

5. Ask questions

Sind Sie ... (= Are you) can be used for a lot of things: where you come from, state of health, name etc.

1/10

*Sind Sie **aus Amerika**?*
1. aus Amerika
2. krank
3. Herr Schroeder
4. aus Italien
5. Frau Krause
6. nicht krank

Hamburg is the most important city in the north, Munich the most important in the south. In the ICE or Intercity Express, a modern high-speed train, the journey between the two cities takes 5 hours 35 minutes, which is pretty fast for around 800 kilometres.

Germany is not all that big, but has plenty of variety: in the south the Alps, in the north the sea, and between them low mountain ranges and plains. It is right in the middle of Europe, surrounded by no less than nine neighbours: Denmark, Poland, the Czech Republic, Austria, Switzerland, France, Luxembourg, Belgium and the Netherlands. The peoples of Europe have migrated through Germany since time immemorial and left their mark: terrible wars followed by periods of peace, wilful destruction and lively cultural exchange. Many people have come to Germany and contributed to the knowledge and artistic life of the country.

Today Germany is one of the seven major industrial powers in the world. Anyone unfamiliar with the country might think it consisted solely of factories and skyscrapers. Industry may be found almost anywhere, but it is concentrated between Duisburg and Dortmund in the Ruhr. Germany also has plenty of unspoilt countryside: 30 % of its surface is covered by forest – coniferous, deciduous or mixed. And 20% consists of agricultural land, although farming can only be kept going if it is heavily subsidized. Skyscrapers, incidentally, are to be found only in Frankfurt, where the banks and insurance companies have their headquarters.

The Germans are people who like to get out and about. Many people who live in towns and cities use the weekend to go out into the countryside and get some exercise. Some also do this to give themselves an excuse to go for a beer or a glass of wine afterwards.

3 What do you do?

When people meet for the first time, they start by finding something out about each other. Some are not particularly curious, and it's enough for them to learn the other person's name. Others want to know what the other person does, if possible also how much money he or she earns, whether he or she is married or still available, has children or debts. Mr Muller asks Ms Krug, *Was machen Sie?* (= What do you do?) The question is ambiguous in German, and can also be understood as "What are you doing right now?" He reformulates his question: *Was arbeiten Sie?* (= What is your job?) But Ms Krug doesn't want to give a direct answer and is vague in her replies: *Ich arbeite für eine Zeitung* (= I work for a newspaper), and *Ich arbeite am Computer* (= I work at the computer). So we don't know whether she's an editor or a secretary. Incidentally, when you meet somebody you shouldn't immediately ask what they do. And you certainly shouldn't ask them what they earn!

was	what
machen	to do
verstehen	to understand
arbeiten	to work
für	for
eine Zeitung	a newspaper
Journalist	journalist
Fotograf	photographer
am Computer	at the computer

Miniconjugation

ich mache   I do
Sie machen   you do

ich verstehe   I understand
Sie verstehen you understand

ich arbeite   I work
Sie arbeiten you work

Was machen Sie?	What do you do?
Ich verstehe nicht ...	I don't understand.
Ja, was arbeiten Sie?	Well, what is your job?
Ich arbeite für eine Zeitung.	I work for a newspaper.
Sehr schön, Frau Krug.	Very nice, Ms Krug.
Ja, das ist sehr schön.	Yes, it is very nice.
Sind Sie Journalistin?	Are you a journalist?
Nein, Herr Muller.	No, Mr Muller.
Sind Sie Fotografin?	Are you a photographer?
Nein.	No.
Was sind Sie?	What are you?
Ich arbeite am Computer.	I work at the computer.

Mr Muller is curious, he wants to know what Ms Krug does for a living.

Did you notice?

A woman is a *Journalistin* or *Fotografin*. Usually when it is a woman being talked about, *in* is added to the end of the masculine word for the occupation concerned.

Some easy questions

Verstehen Sie? Do you understand?
Arbeiten Sie? Do you work?
Kommen Sie? Are you coming?
Ist das schön? Is that nice?

Normally, as in English, the person comes first, then the verb: *Sie kommen*. In a question it is the other way round: *Kommen Sie?*

The easiest translation

1. Sort into pairs

1.	Zeitung	a ■	what is your job
2.	ich verstehe	b ■	what do you do
3.	was machen Sie	c ■	I understand
4.	was arbeiten Sie	d ■	newspaper

The second easiest translation, as it's always harder to translate in the other direction - into the foreign language.

2. Give the English translation

1. sehr schön *very nice* _____   2. Zeitung _____
3. Computer _____   4. ich verstehe nicht _____
5. was machen Sie? _____   6. ich arbeite _____
7. Entschuldigung _____   8. woher kommen Sie? _____

Watch out! The answers always sound rather similar, but in the context they are very different.

3. Which answer is right?

1/12

1. Was machen Sie?   a ■ Ich bin krank.
                          b ■ Ich bin Fotograf.

2. Woher kommen Sie?   a ■ Ich komme aus Brasilien.
                          b ■ Ich bin Journalist.

3. Wie heißen Sie?   a ■ Ich bin Fotograf.
                          b ■ Ich heiße Becker.

4. Verstehen Sie?   a ■ Nein, ich verstehe nicht.
                          b ■ Nein, ich komme nicht.

Change the verb from the third to the first person. Think back to the miniconjugation: with *ich* the verb has no -*n* at the end.

4. You → I

1. Sie machen → ich *mache*   2. Sie arbeiten → ich _____
3. Sie sind → ich _____   4. Sie verstehen → ich _____
5. Sie kommen → ich _____   6. Sie wissen → ich _____

raten	....	to guess
mal	....	just
Ingenieur	....	engineer
auch	....	also
auch nicht	....	not ... either
Student	....	student
ich weiß	....	I know
interessant	....	interesting

Write the words and their translation on pieces of paper. Sometimes it helps to put the ones you just can't get into your head in your wallet!

Herr Muller?	....	Mr Muller?
Ja?	....	Yes?
Was machen Sie?	....	What do you do?
Raten Sie mal.	....	Have a guess.
Sind Sie Journalist?	....	Are you a journalist?
Nein.	....	No.
Ingenieur?	....	An engineer?
Auch nicht.	....	Not that either.
Sind Sie vielleicht Student?	.....	Are you perhaps a student?
Oh neiiiin, hahahah.	....	Oh nooo, hahaha.
Ich weiß!	....	I know!
Ja?	....	Yes?
Sie sind Fotograf.	....	You're a photographer.
Ja, ich bin Fotograf.	....	Yes, I'm a photographer.
Ist das interessant?	....	Is that interesting?
Ja, sehr interessant.	....	Yes, very interesting.

Now Ms Krug wants to know what Mr Muller does. He doesn't want to tell her right off and says *Raten Sie mal* (= Have a guess.). *Mal* is one of those German words that don't really mean any-thing. In this case *Raten Sie* (= Guess) on its own, would sound a little stark. *Mal* is actually the abbreviation of *einmal* (= once).

Ich weiß in fact comes from *wissen* (= to know) and *ich bin* from *sein* (= to be). Unfortunately not all verbs are regular! But there's no language which is complete-ly regular. Only artificial lan-guages such as Esperanto or computer-programming lan-guages …

1. Sort into pairs

1.	auch nicht	a ■	very interesting
2.	vielleicht	b ■	have a guess
3.	ich weiß	c ■	I know
4.	sehr interessant	d ■	very nice
5.	sehr schön	e ■	not … either
6.	raten Sie mal	f ■	maybe

2. What are you?

1/14

Was sind Sie? - *Ich bin* **Fotograf.**
1. Fotograf   2. Journalist   3. Student
4. Ingenieur   5. Amerikaner

3. Find the right answer

1. Ist das interessant?   a ■ Ja, ein bisschen.
                          b ■ Ich arbeite.
2. Verstehen Sie?   a ■ Ja, alles in Ordnung.
                    b ■ Ja, das bin ich.
3. Sind Sie vielleicht Journalistin? a ■ Nein, das ist schön.
                          b ■ Nein, ich arbeite nicht.
4. Sind Sie Ingenieur?   a ■ Nein, das ist schön.
                          b ■ Raten Sie mal.

4. What about the women?

1. der Journalist   die *Journalistin* _____
2. der Student   die _____
3. der Fotograf   die _____
4. der Ingenieur   die _____

5. I → you

1. ich heiße   Sie *heißen*   2. ich komme   Sie _____
3. ich arbeite   Sie _____   4. ich verstehe   Sie _____
5. ich mache   Sie _____   6. ich bin   Sie _____

In many languages *Deutschland* (Germany) is named after one of the many different Germanic peoples, e.g. the Teutons, where the word *deutsch* comes from, or the Alemannians, where the name for Germany comes from in most of the Romance languages. Originally the Germanic peoples came from the area between southern Sweden, Denmark and North Germany.

The Frankish Empire (the Franks were another Germanic tribe) was created in Europe at the time of the migration of the peoples. Under Charles the Great in 800 AD, this kingdom consisted of Germany, France, the northern part of Italy and parts of Spain. In Strasbourg, now the seat of the European Court, the Empire was divided in 842 into an eastern and western part, which eventually became Germany and France.

For a thousand years, what is now Germany was split up into numerous kingdoms, princedoms and free cities (Hamburg, Bremen, Lübeck). It was only under Chancellor Bismarck after the Franco-Prussian war in 1870–71 that all this was united and Germany became a proper country. Berlin was made the capital, and in the 1920s became the centre of an interesting cultural life.

Germany's darkest hours were the World War it provoked in 1914–18 and in particular the Nazi era from 1933 to 1945, when Hitler dreamed of a Greater Germany stretching from the Atlantic to the Urals, invaded other countries and attempted, through persecution and mass murder, to eradicate Jews, gypsies, socialists, communists, homosexuals and other minorities.

Charles the Great resided mainly in Aachen and in Ingelheim am Rhein. In Rome he was crowned Emperor of the Holy Roman Empire.

The last German emperor, Wilhelm II, had to abdicate after Germany lost the war in 1918. He went into exile in Holland.

The first Federal Chancellor, in 1949, was Konrad Adenauer, who remained in office until 1963. Only Helmut Kohl has been Chancellor for a longer period.

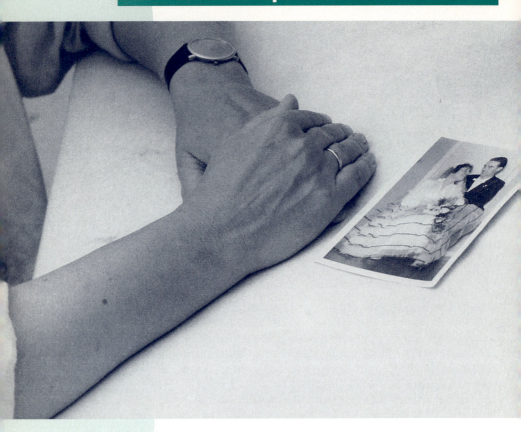

When you're getting to know somebody, at some point the conversation turns to more personal things. Sometimes – when for example the man's wife has just run off with the milkman – the question *Sind Sie verheiratet?* (= Are you married?) might be quite the wrong thing to say. Politics is another subject where you might get into deep water. Not everyone is tolerant of other people's opinions. An initial liking can soon change to antipathy all because the other person is for or against Gadhafi or the American President.

Our Mr Muller proceeds cautiously and first asks a question which everyone usually answers with "yes". *Ich habe eine Frage* (= I have a question). Only now does he pluck up courage to ask whether Ms Krug is married. If this question is asked early on by a man, it usually means he finds the woman attractive. But be careful, this question can be taken the wrong way. When it's a bit much for Ms Krug she gets round it with *Sie sind aber neugierig!* (= You're very curious).

ich habe	. . . .	I have
eine Frage	. . . .	a question
verheiratet	. . . .	married
Ihr	. . . .	your
Mann	. . . .	husband, man
mein	. . . .	my
aber	. . . .	but
neugierig	. . . .	curious

Have you ever thought about the best way to learn vocabulary? There's no patent recipe. Some people learn better from reading and writing things down, while others prefer to listen and say the words out loud. But however you do it, the most important thing is to repeat the words often enough to store them reliably and if possible forever on your brain's hard disk.

Frau Krug?	. . . .	Ms Krug?
Ja.	. . . .	Yes.
Ich habe eine Frage.	. . . .	I have a question.
Ja, bitte?	. . . .	Yes?
Sind Sie verheiratet?	. . . .	Are you married?
Ja, ich bin verheiratet.	. . . .	Yes, I'm married.
Und Ihr Mann?	. . . .	And your husband?
Mein Mann ist in Amerika.	. . . . . .	My husband is in America.
Sehr schön.	. . . .	Very nice.
Na ja …		Well …
Ist Ihr Mann Ingenieur?	. . . .	Is your husband an engineer?
Sie sind aber neugierig!!!	. . . .	You're very curious!!!

Mr Muller and Ms Krug are asking each other questions that are a bit more personal. You could almost say they are flirting a little …

Aber means "but". It is often used to express surprise and astonishment, or is used for extra emphasis. For example a woman given a beautiful bouquet of roses might say: *Die sind aber schön* (= These are really lovely).

Minigrammar:
Possessives

ich	→	*mein*
Sie	→	*Ihr*

Note the capital letters used for *Sie* und *Ihr*. This is important in order to avoid mix-ups: *sie* with a small "s", for example, means "she".

1. Translate into German

If there are three or more words you don't know, then there's only one thing for it: go back one page, open your eyes wide and look again.

1. curious _ _ _ _ _ _ _ _
2. married _ _ _ _ _ _ _ _ _ _ _
3. question _ _ _ _ _
4. engineer _ _ _ _ _ _ _
5. really _ _ _ _ _ _ _ _
6. but _ _ _ _
7. bad _ _ _ _ _ _ _
8. ill _ _ _ _ _

2. Do you have a ...?

Here all the words are feminine, which is why it's always eine (not ein).

*Haben Sie **eine Frage?***

1. die Frage
2. die Zeitung
3. die Frau
4. die Pizza
5. die Bank
6. die Information

3. Sort into matching pairs

Which answer belongs to which question?

1. Sind Sie neugierig?
2. Sind Sie verheiratet?
3. Sind Sie Ingenieur?
4. Sind Sie Herr Möllers?
5. Sind Sie krank?

a ■ Nein, alles in Ordnung.
b ■ Nein, mein Name ist Müller.
c ■ Ja, sehr neugierig.
d ■ Ja, mein Mann ist aber in Berlin.
e ■ Nein, ich arbeite nicht.

4. That's not my ...

Here all the words are masculine or neuter, so it's always mein (not meine).

*Das ist nicht **mein Problem**.*

1. das Problem
2. der Mann
3. das Leben
4. der Computer
5. das Foto
6. das Radio

leben	....	live
alleine	....	alone
eine Freundin	....	a (girl-)friend
nur	....	only
manchmal	....	sometimes
zwei	....	two
Stress	....	stress

Depending on who's speaking, *Freundin* can be just a female friend, or a girlfriend.

Der Stress – another international word. And an international phenomenon.

Ich habe auch eine Frage.	......	I have a question, too.
Ja, Frau Krug?	....	Yes, Mrs Krug?
Sind Sie verheiratet?	....	Are you married?
Nein, das bin ich nicht.	....	No, I'm not.
Leben Sie alleine?	....	Do you live alone?
Nein, ich habe eine Freundin.	...	No, I have a girl-friend.
Nur eine, Herr Muller?	....	Only one, Mr Muller?
Ehhhm, manchmal zwei.	....	Errm, sometimes two.
Sehr interessant.	....	Very interesting.
Nein, das ist Stress!	....	No, that's stress!

Mrs Krug wants to know what's what this time. Mr Muller even gets a bit embarrassed by her questions and says *Ehhm*.

Incidentally: *haben* takes the accusative. What is that? You don't need to know yet, so we'll give you an example instead:
ich habe **ein-** Problem
        (das Problem)
ich habe **ein-e** Freundin
        (die Freundin)
ich habe **ein-en** Freund
        (der Freund)
More about this later.

Minigrammar:
Three articles

definite		indefinite
der	masculine	*ein*
die	feminine	*eine*
das	neuter	*ein*

1. Which answer is right?

You know this exercise. It's not that easy as all the answers sound possible. You'll have to look closely to pick out the right one.

1. Leben Sie alleine?
   a ■ Ja, ich habe eine Frau.
   b ■ Ja, ich bin nicht verheiratet.

2. Arbeiten Sie am Computer?
   a ■ Nein, ich bin Fotograf.
   b ■ Nein, ich arbeite alleine.

3. Haben Sie eine Frage?
   a ■ Ja, wie heißen Sie?
   b ■ Ja, ich habe eine Frau.

4. Sind Sie neugierig?
   a ■ Ja, ich habe eine Frage.
   b ■ Ja, ich bin krank.

2. A little German translation

Congratulations, if you get this translation right. It's the first proper translation – we've only asked for words before. Here it's whole sentences.

1. I work by myself. _____
2. Mr Schulz is curious. _____
3. Fred is ill. _____
4. I've got a problem. _____
5. That's wonderful. _____

3. What's missing?

If you get number 2 right, 3 will be child's play.

1. I've got a girlfriend.   Ich habe eine _ _ _ _ _ _ _ _ .
2. I've got a problem.   Ich habe ein _ _ _ _ _ _ _ .
3. Do you have a question?   Haben Sie eine _ _ _ _ _ ?
4. You have a newspaper.   Sie haben eine _ _ _ _ _ _ _ .
5. You are under stress.   Sie haben _ _ _ _ _ _ .

4. Which is the odd one out?

This is something that requires a little thought again. In every group of four words there is one that does not belong. So you need to find the abstract category that applies to three of the four words.

1. Mann - Frau - Leben - Herr
2. Freundin - Student - Ingenieur - Fotograf
3. schön - schlimm - interessant - wunderbar
4. arbeiten - haben - bisschen - kommen
5. Zeitung - Computer - Radio - Musik

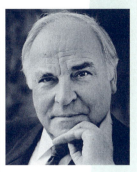

The most important historical event in Germany since 1945 has been reunification. The people in the GDR felt too restricted and wanted more freedom. A crucial phase of the revolution began when thousands of GDR citizens barricaded themselves in the Embassy of the Federal Republic in Prague and others crossed the Hungarian-Austrian border into the "free West", in other words simply ran away from home. Revolutionary fervour took hold in their home country and, with their non-violent protests, the people of the GDR forced their government to its knees. The 9th November 1989 marks the fall of the wall in Berlin. On this day the Brandenburg Gate was opened: East and West Germans celebrated, proclaiming *Wir sind ein Volk* (= We are one nation) and fell into one another's arms.

Not for long, as it soon became apparent that East and West Germans are unequal partners in the new marriage: one part of the country simply has more money than the other. West Germans have often made themselves unpopular because of their know-all, arrogant manner when they visit the East. And *Ossis* are not treated very sympathetically because the *Wessis* feel that they are having to pay for the reconstruction in the East.

The capital

The official capital of Germany is once again Berlin. But most of the government and the Parliament are still in Bonn. It will be a few years before all the ministries have moved to Berlin. There is quite a bit of criticism of the move: it is said that it will cost a total of 8,000,000,000 DM. That's eight hundred billion pfennigs.

Bundesrepublik Deutschland

Bundesrepublik means Federal Republic. There are 16 federal *Länder*, which can make some of their decisions independently of the Federal Government in Bonn/Berlin.

Don't get them mixed up: Aussies and *Ossis* (East Germans).

1. Which is right?

1. German is spoken by
   a ■ 4,500,000 people.
   b ■ 45,000,000 people.
   c ■ over 100,000,000 people.
2. Germany has
   a ■ large areas of forest, approx. 30%.
   b ■ large areas of desert, approx. 50%.
   c ■ large areas of water, approx. 80%.
3. The country is surrounded by
   a ■ six other nations.
   b ■ nine other nations.
   c ■ twelve other nations.
4. There are skyscrapers in
   a ■ every German city with a population of over a million.
   b ■ only in Zürich.
   c ■ only in Frankfurt.
5. Germany existed as a complete country
   a ■ from 800 – 1918.
   b ■ from 1492 – 1789.
   c ■ from 1871 – 1945 and from 1989 on.
6. Between East and West Germans
   a ■ everything is now harmonious.
   b ■ there are a lot of problems.
   c ■ stands the Berlin wall.

2. Answers and questions

1. Nein, ich bin Ingenieur.
2. Sie sind aber neugierig.
3. Nein, ich bin verheiratet.
4. Ich arbeite nicht.
5. Mein Name ist Schneider.
6. Ich bin aus Österreich.

a ■ Leben Sie alleine?
b ■ Was machen Sie?
c ■ Sind Sie vielleicht Student?
d ■ Sind Sie verheiratet?
e ■ Woher kommen Sie?
f ■ Wie heißen Sie?

3. Multiple choice

Only one of the little words will fit the gap to give you a meaningful sentence. You can make nonsense sentences in the following translation section.

1. Wie _____ Sie?
   a ◼ arbeite
   b ◼ heißen
   c ◼ Name
2. Ich komme _____ Hamburg.
   a ◼ nein
   b ◼ aus
   c ◼ bin
3. Mein Name _____ Rolf Kaul.
   a ◼ ist
   b ◼ habe
   c ◼ heißen
4. Woher _____ Sie?
   a ◼ bin
   b ◼ aus
   c ◼ kommen
5. Ich bin _____ bisschen krank.
   a ◼ ein
   b ◼ nein
   c ◼ danke
6. Ich _____ für eine Zeitung.
   a ◼ arbeiten
   b ◼ habe
   c ◼ arbeite

4. Sense and nonsense

1. My name is student.
2. I have an excuse me.
3. Is everything interesting in Berlin?
4. Life is so ill!
5. It's not a problem, Mrs Newspaper.
6. I understand maybe.

If you play with words when you are learning a language, it will come easier. Even if you are asked to translate nonsense, you must have the appropriate words ready. Please translate literally from English into German. You know all the words, but the sense in which they are being used is new and will maybe tickle your imagination too.

A. u. Straßburger C. Draiser-130a	36 67 06
A. Göttelmann-42b	8 22 00
A. Leibniz-51	67 69 34
A. Walpoden-23	22 18 51
A.-M. Leibniz-	67 23 40
Albrecht Dipl.Ing. Tucholskyweg 44	7 23 93
Alfred	69 06 29
Andreas Obere Zahlbacher-40	5 58 20
Annette Draiser-8	3 59 37
Arno Weintor-22	22 90 36
Axel Bopp-46	67 27 05
B. u. M. Gemeindehohl 34	47 77 69
B. Kreyßig-2	60 41 76
C. F. Walpoden-1	23 21 20
Ch. Ufer-25	23 26 47
Charlotte Weingarten-1	3 44 24
Christa Westring 32	68 55 14
Claus Westring 283	68 38 10
D.	63 85 99
D. Am Kirchborn 16c	47 06 43
Dagmar Jakob-Dieterich-13	61 49 68
Dieter Jll-15	67 19 25
Elisabeth u. Beutler Ute	36 10 65
herrngasse 15	
Eike	67 37 36
Erdmute u. Eckhard	59 33 73
echenberg 4	
Ernst-D. Josefs-44	67 08 93
Fritz Elsa-Brändström-67	68 68 34
Harald u. Görgen-Krüger Cornelia	50 76 86
Hartmut Urologe	88 31 60
eimer Weg 39	
ger Hartmut	☎ 22 91 88
t für Urologie	
ße Bleiche 2	
Hartmut Rhein-20	22 08 94
Heidi u. Jochen Riesling-58	59 39 33
Heike u. Hardy	8 63 67
Heinz u. Therese Hecker-5	68 25 03
Heinz Nack-5	67 04 30

Krummel M. Am Hipperich 105	68 49 31
Krümmel T. u. Siebecker S.	83 24 30
Langgasse 21	
Krümmelbein Brunolf Barbarossaring 9	67 93 90
Krümpel Verlag KG Curt-Goetz-31	☎ 47 41 05
Priv.	47 71 12
Krümpelmann Justus Prof. Dr.	3 49 32
Am Eselsweg 30	
Krützfeldt Hans-J. Schuster-56	☎ 22 02 75
Kruft Hartmut Am Mühlbach 19	36 96 45
Krug	33 83 38
Krug A. Hoch-5	36 14 32
Krug C.	88 23 04
Krug Fritz Landwehrweg 46	5 50 30
Krug Georg Lindenschmit-21	22 08 70
Krug Günther Rechtsanwalt	22 22 94
Emmerich-Josef-18	
Krug Günther Friedrich-Schneider-10	5 50 77
Krug H. E. Dr.	83 20 00
Krug Harald Hoch-5	33 86 12
Krug Hayo u. Poppe Jutta Groß-Gerauer-82	8 76 87
Krug Helmut Flachsmarkt-26	22 88 76
Krug Helmut BrauMstr. Sertoriusring 15	47 10 77
Krug Holger	
Autotelefon	Fu 0 16 13 63 09 04
Krug Jakob Thomas-Mann-7	3 11 83
Krug Johann B. Immelmann-2	4 27 46
Krug Karl-H. Albrecht-Dürer-1	3 41 74
Krug Klaus Zedernweg 18	36 34 28
Krug Lin	36 51 72
Krug Ludwig Herderpl. 6	47 43 75
Krug Maike An der Kirschhecke 16	36 55 74
Krug Manfred Finther Land-91	47 32 71
Krug Norbert Van-Gogh-10	7 23 32
Krug P.	61 44 31
Krug Peter Hintere Christofsgasse 5	23 31 79
Krug Peter Dr. u. Eva Sandmühlweg 17b	47 61 73
Krug Philippine Wilhelms-32	33 15 41
Krug Robert Bäckerei Elbe-5	4 18 36
Krug T. u. Hüser M. Am Kirchborn 20e	47 56 25
Krug W.	67 32 84
Krug Wilfried Große Langgasse 9	22 15 77

(Münchfeld)	
priv.	**50 40 22**
Kruschel Alfred Hafen-8c	67 41 20
Kruschke Horst Hermann-Löns-39	4 06 96
Kruse André u. Hannah Pfädchengasse 7	47 75 78
Kruse Fritz Pfarrer-Dorn-25	36 31 89
Kruse G. u. Schmitt I. Forster-16	61 17 95
Kruse Gerhard u. Ilse Forster-9	67 20 26
Kruse Günter Kelten-24	8 55 43
Kruse H.	32 04 36
Kruse Harald Rochus-6	23 00 73
Kruse Heinz Dr.med. Heidesheimer-41a	4 19 93
Kruse Peter Vogelsberg-65a	59 26 04
Kruse Petra Hans-Böckler-45	36 39 13
Kruse R. Kernerweg 26	50 85 36
Kruse-Ribbat Eva	47 49 53
Kruse Steffen Im Münchfeld 33	37 15 47
Krusenotto E.-M. Mosel-9	63 85 97
Krusenotto Helmut Ing.	5 23 95
Am Fort Elisabeth 5	
KRUSIUS	**4 61 98**
Estriche-Parkett	
Bodenbeläge	
Heidesheimer Str. 30	
Krusius Mathias Heidesheimer-30	4 32 70
Krusius Peter M. Heidesheimer-30b	4 13 63
Kruska Siegfried Hindenburg-43	61 17 64
Kruth Herbert Parseval-7	68 91 02
Kruth Fritz Parseval-7	68 95 21
Krutka Irene Am Taubertsberg 4	38 17 04
Krys Siegfried u. Weber Magda	23 59 35
Am Brand 22	
Krystanczyk Gerhard Am Leitgraben 23	88 13 03
Krzanowski Antoni Südring 34	36 96 03
Krzeminski Henryk	☎ 5 99 85
An den Mühlwegen 34	
Krzeminski Stanislaw	68 39 53
An der Bruchspitze 49	
Krictek Rolf Rheinallee 27	67 95 33

Kublick Dr.	
Kublun Hans Taunus-47	
Kubot Herbert Barbarossaring 23	
Kubotsch Anna Nelkenweg 12	
Kubotsch Josef Uhland-14	
Kubotsch Willy P. Katzenberg 28	
Kubura Branko Mosel-19	
Kubura Mirko Schubert-22	
Kuch Herbert Dijon-79	
Kucharski Antoni Dresdener-38	
Kuchel B. Berliner-5	
Kuchel S.	
Kuchel S. Heidelbergerfaßgasse 16	
Kuchenbäcker Christel Raimundi-27	
Kuchenbäcker Dirk Im Münchfeld 26	
Kuchenbauer S.	
Kuchenbecker Alfred Langenbeck-3	
Kuchenbecker Angela u. Kathrin	
Kuchenbecker M. Langenbeck-32	
Kuchenbecker R.	
Kuchenbecker S.	
Kuchenbecker Thomas	
Im Münchfeld 33	
Kuchenbuch, Dieter	
Kuchenbuch sen. G. u. L.	
Am Fort Gonsenheim 104	
Kuchenbuch Karsten Werra-8	
Kuchenmeister Josef	
Kuchenmeister K. u. G. Am Gautor 3	
Kuchfeld Ria Tönges-2	
Kuck Anneliese Van-Gogh-4	
Kuck Patricia Van-Gogh-4	
Kuck U. Aspelt-7	
Kucki Helmut Elisabethen-23	
Kucklei	
Kuckuck Anneliese Westring 46	
Kuckuk A. u. W.	

It's not very nice to call someone *eine Null* (= a dead loss).

There are many people in the world who cannot read or write, but who can do arithmetic. Numbers are more important for survival than letters, perhaps because numbers order, measure and determine things. With letters and words there is a certain flexibility, but you have to take numbers as they come. A thousand marks are a thousand marks.

In this age of communication, people define themselves by numbers: *Ihre Telefonnummer bitte?* (= What's your telephone number please?) Sometimes people are cross when you are not at home and don't answer the phone, demanding to know why you haven't got an answering machine. People are obsessed by the idea that they must always be reachable. If you are sitting in the train or in the cinema and one of these self-important people is talking so loudly on his mobile that everyone can hear every single word, it can really get on your nerves. Especially when you have to listen to such banalities as, "Darling, look in the fridge, there must still be a bit of cheese or something in there."

Telephoning can also be important when you are first getting to know someone: *Kann ich Sie anrufen?* (= Can I call you?) A great deal can depend on the answer …

kann .... can
anrufen .... to call
natürlich .... of course
die Telefonnummer .... telephone number
brauchen .... to need
die Vorwahl .... area code
morgen .... tomorrow
um neun .... at nine (o'clock)

A verb with a prefix:
anrufen (= to call)

ich rufe ... an   I call
Sie rufen ... an   You call

Important verbs

ich brauche   I need
Sie brauchen   you need
ich kann   I can
Sie können   you can

**An easy lesson
in telling the time:**

um eins   at one (o'clock)
um sechs   at six (o'clock)
um zehn   at ten (o'clock)

Kann ich Sie anrufen? .... Can I call you?
Natürlich. .... Of course.
Was ist Ihre Telefonnummer? ... What's your telephone
                             number?
Ich habe die 3-2-8-4-5-1-6. ..... It's 3-2-8-4-5-1-6.
Wie bitte? .... Pardon?
Drei-zwei-acht-vier-fünf-eins-
sechs. .... Three-two-eight-four-five-one
                             six.
In Frankfurt? .... In Frankfurt?
Ja, Sie brauchen keine Vorwahl.   Yes, you don't need the area code.
Gut, ich rufe morgen an. .... Good, I'll call you tomorrow.
Können Sie um neun anrufen? .. Can you call at nine?
Kein Problem. .... No problem.

The numbers *zwei* (= two)
und *zehn* (= ten) show you
how German and English
are related.

Numbers are very practical. Imagine if you had to write not 1,234, but one thousand two hundred and thirty-four (*eintausendzwei-hundertundvierunddreißig*) every time …

1. Sort into pairs

1.	sechs	5.	vier	a ▪	5	e ▪	9
2.	acht	6.	sieben	b ▪	3	f ▪	1
3.	neun	7.	fünf	c ▪	6	g ▪	4
4.	eins	8.	drei	d ▪	8	h ▪	7

Some people say *plus* (= plus) instead of *und*, and *gleich* (= equals) instead of *ist*. We hope that the arithmetic here is not too difficult.

2. Fill in

Zwei und drei ist fünf.

1. $2 + 3 = ...$?   _ _ _ _ und _ _ _ _ ist _ _ _ _.
2. $1 + 7 = ...$?   _ _ _ _ und _ _ _ _ _ _ ist _ _ _ _.
3. $4 + 2 = ...$?   _ _ _ _ und _ _ _ _ ist _ _ _ _ _.
4. $5 + 2 = ...$?   _ _ _ _ und _ _ _ _ ist _ _ _ _ _ _.
5. $3 + 6 = ...$?   _ _ _ _ und _ _ _ _ _ ist _ _ _ _.

Another accusative

Remember that *haben* takes the accusative, which means that when it's followed by a masculine word like *Computer*, *-en* is added to *ein* to make it *einen Computer*. The definite article changes as follows: *der → den*.

3. What do you need?

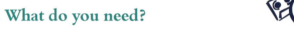

Was brauchen Sie? – Ich brauche ein Telefon.

1. ein Telefon
2. eine Zeitung
3. einen Computer
4. ein Foto
5. eine Freundin
6. Ihren Namen
7. Ihre Telefonnummer
8. die Vorwahl von Berlin

4. Can I …?

This question always sounds polite:
Kann ich …? (= Can I?)
Even more polite is:
Kann ich bitte …?
(= Can I … please?)

Kann ich telefonieren?

1. telefonieren
2. am Computer arbeiten
3. eine Zeitung haben
4. morgen kommen
5. das verstehen
6. in Hamburg leben
7. mal raten
8. Ihre Telefonnummer haben

5. What is the next number?

Simply write out the number which follows. A good way to practise numbers is when going upstairs: count them out loud as you go. But just imagine the lift wasn't working and you had to walk up to the 13th floor, counting all the way …

sieben, acht.

1. sieben _ _ _ _
2. fünf _ _ _ _ _
3. eins _ _ _ _
4. neun _ _ _ _
5. vier _ _ _ _
6. drei _ _ _ _
7. sechs _ _ _ _ _ _

sprechen	to speak
glauben	to think, to believe
das Zimmer	room
einen Moment	just a moment
hören Sie	listen
er	he
im Moment	at the moment
hier	here
zurückrufen	to call back
Danke schön	thank you very much

Mouth:

Ich spreche I speak
Sie sprechen you speak

Ear:

ich höre I listen
Sie hören you listen

Head:

ich glaube I think
Sie glauben you think

In this context *glauben* means "to think", but it is also the word for "to believe".

Hallo, Hotel Gutenberg?	Hallo, is that the Hotel Gutenberg?
Ja, bitte?	Yes, can I help you?
Kann ich Herrn Muller sprechen?	Can I speak to Mr Muller?
Herr Muller?	Mr Muller?
Ja, ich glaube Zimmer drei zwei vier.	Yes, I think (he's in) room three two four.
Einen Moment bitte.	Just a moment, please.
Hören Sie bitte	Listen ...
Ja?	Yes?
Herr Muller ist im Moment nicht hier.	Mr Muller's not here at the moment.
Wirklich nicht?	Really?
Nein, kann er Sie zurückrufen?	No, can he call you back?
Natürlich.	Of course.
Ihr Name bitte?	Your name please?
Ich bin Frau Krug.	I'm Mrs Krug.
Und Ihre Telefonnummer?	And your telephone number?
Das ist die 3-2-8-4-5-1-6.	It's 3-2-8-4-5-1-6.
Danke schön.	Thank you very much.

Einen Moment bitte (= Just a moment, please) is the most frequently heard sentence on the telephone. Unfortunately it is often then another half hour before you are connected with the person you want to speak to.

Rufen – call

anrufen = to call (phone)
zurückrufen = to call back
Did you notice? *zurück* = back. *Zurückkommen* (= to come back) is constructed the same way.

1. Find the translation

1. Sprechen Sie!
2. Hören Sie!
3. Arbeiten Sie!
4. Raten Sie!
5. Kommen Sie!

a ■ Guess!
b ■ Work!
c ■ Speak!
d ■ Come!
e ■ Listen!

2. Which is the right answer?

1. Können Sie um acht anrufen?
   a ■ Ja, natürlich.
   b ■ Ich bin um acht hier.
2. Kann ich Frau Mayer sprechen?
   a ■ Nein, Frau Mayer ist hier.
   b ■ Nein, Frau Mayer ist nicht hier.
3. Brauche ich eine Vorwahl?
   a ■ Nein, das ist meine Telefonnummer.
   b ■ Nein, die Nummer ist in Frankfurt.
4. Kann ich zurückrufen?
   a ■ Ich habe ein Telefon.
   b ■ Nein, ich bin nicht zu Hause.

3. Give the German for it:

1. at eight o'clock   _ _   _ _ _ _
2. the room   _ _ _   _ _ _ _ _ _
3. to call back   _ _ _ _ _ _ _ _ _ _
4. he   _ _
5. of course   _ _ _ _ _ _ _ _
6. tomorrow   _ _ _ _ _
7. the area code   _ _ _   _ _ _ _ _ _

4. Read the telephone number in German

1. 3 - 2 - 1 - 6 - 8 - 9
2. 7 - 9 - 2 - 1 - 5 - 4
3. 6 - 8 - 2 - 4 - 1 - 6
4. 9 - 2 - 1 - 8 - 5 - 6
5. 9 - 8 - 2 - 5 - 7 - 3
6. 7 - 5 - 3 - 1 - 9 - 7
7. 2 - 4 - 6 - 8 - 2 - 4
8. 1 - 2 - 9 - 8 - 6 - 5

5. Ask questions

*Können Sie **morgen anrufen?***
1. morgen anrufen
2. gut Deutsch sprechen
3. um neun kommen
4. die Arbeit machen
5. das verstehen

Nowadays if you don't fancy going out, you can stay at home for the rest of your life. Provided you have a telephone. With this you can order anything from pizzas to bed linen, do all your banking (in German it is actually called *Telefonbanking*) and call an ambulance or have (telephone-)sex. If you have a fax machine as well, you can also write letters without having to go and buy stamps or go to the postbox. If anything has made life convenient, it's the telephone.

The telephone saves time. There is an awful lot that can be done by telephone, so that we no longer have to go in person to the inland revenue office or the council's waste disposal department. The telephone saves petrol, because you no longer have to get in your car and go to see your best friend when there is a major problem you absolutely must talk to her about. And the telephone saves money, because you no longer have to go to a café in order just to talk.

A lot of social contact takes place over the telephone, and there are people who suffer from "telephonitis", spending hours at a time on the phone. Customs have changed: once you never called anyone at home between one and three, because that was the sacred rest period after lunch. Today nobody keeps to this, and you can telephone anywhere at any time. If you watch some of the most important debates in the German parliament on television, you will see that some members of parliament are not listening at all, but talking away on the phone.

Telephone boxes

Recognizable by their dull designer-grey sides and mauve-and-red roof. Most public telephones only take cards. If, however, you have a card and have to make an urgent call, then it's bound to be a coin-operated box and you won't have the right coins on you. Telephoning is expensive from hotels and at the post office.

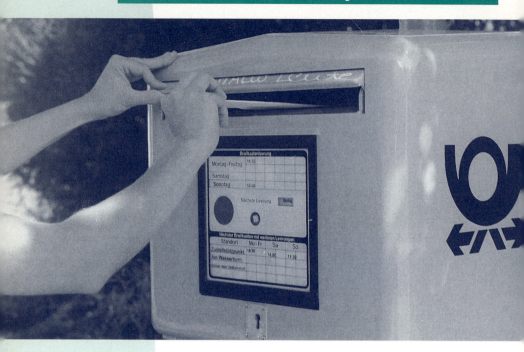

More numbers

11	*elf*	16	*sechzehn*
12	*zwölf*	17	*siebzehn*
13	*dreizehn*	18	*achtzehn*
14	*vierzehn*	19	*neunzehn*
15	*fünfzehn*	20	*zwanzig*

Postal charges

There are two rates for cards and letters, depending on whether they are being sent within Germany and Europe or to other continents.

Parcels of all sizes are very expensive, with five different charge zones:
1. Germany,
2. Europe,
3. USA,
4. South America/Africa/Asia,
5. Australia/ New Zealand etc.

Schreib mal wieder (= Drop somebody a line) is the post office's advertising slogan to encourage people to write to each other more often. The post office badly needs those extra letters, as writing has gone out of fashion. Perhaps because it takes so much longer than a quick phone call. People who have just fallen in love or who live a long way away from one another still write letters. And holidaymakers write, but not too much, not more than a nice postcard, just to prove that they really are abroad.

So *Ich brauche Briefmarken* (= I need some stamps) is a sentence that is useful when you are travelling. You can only get stamps, by the way, at the post office. And since the post office is usually shut when you most need it, there is a yellow vending machine outside which will spit out something that you can stick on a letter in return for a few coins. *Münzwertzeichendrucker* (= coin-operated stamp printer) is the name of the machine, which produces a type of stamp that hurts every collector's sensibilities. If you want to give the person you are writing to a pleasant surprise, go to the counter and buy some attractive stamps. These cost exactly the same as the computer products and add something to the look of the letter. There are also charity stamps which cost a bit more and help a good cause.

die Briefmarke	stamp
wie viele?	how many
der Brief	letter
die Postkarte	postcard
die Telefonkarte	phone card
bekommen	to get
das macht ...	that's ...
tut mir Leid ...	sorry ...
wieder	again

A lesson in plurals:

ein Brief	zwei Brief-**e**
eine Briefmarke	zwei Briefmark-**en**
eine Postkarte	zwei Postkart-**en**
eine Telefonkarte	zwei Telefonkart-**en**
wie viel?	wie viel-**e**?

Ja bitte?	Can I help you?
Ich brauche Briefmarken.	I need some stamps.
Wie viele?	How many?
Emmh, für vier Briefe.	Erm, for four letters.
Ist das alles?	Is that all?
Und für vier Postkarten.	And for four postcards.
Vier und vier, das macht acht Mark.	Four and four, that makes eight marks.
Kann ich hier auch Telefonkarten bekommen?	Can I get phone cards here, too?
Natürlich. Wie viele?	Of course. How many?
Eine für zwölf Mark bitte.	One for twelve marks, please.
Acht und zwölf, das macht zwanzig Mark.	Eight and twelve, that's twenty marks.
Oh, ich habe nur zehn Mark.	Oh, I've only got ten marks.
Kein Problem.	No problem.
Tut mir Leid ...	Sorry ...
Kommen Sie bitte morgen wieder.	Come back tomorrow, please.

You can buy pre-stamped ordinary postcards (i.e. not picture postcards) at the post office, too.

Has this ever happened to you: you are out shopping and about to pay when you discover you haven't got enough money with you? Embarrassing ...

1. Can I get … here?

Kann ich hier **Zeitungen** *bekommen?*

1. Zeitungen
2. Briefmarken
3. Postkarten
4. Telefonkarten
5. Hamburger
6. Computer
7. Telefone
8. Radios
9. Probleme

2. Find the right answer

1. Haben Sie Telefonkarten?
   a ■ Nein, tut mir Leid.
   b ■ Ich rufe morgen an.

2. Haben Sie Postkarten?
   a ■ Ich habe nur Briefmarken.
   b ■ Postkarten? Wunderbar!

3. Haben Sie zehn Mark?
   a ■ Ich brauche zehn Mark.
   b ■ Natürlich,
       hier haben Sie zwanzig.

4. Haben Sie Fragen?
   a ■ Tut mir Leid.
   b ■ Ja, eine Frage.

3. Sort into matching pairs

1. der Mann
2. die Frage
3. bitte
4. die Briefmarke
5. Auf Wiedersehen

a ■ der Brief
b ■ Guten Tag
c ■ die Frau
d ■ danke
e ■ das Problem

4. How much is it?

Neun Zeitungen, *das macht* **achtzehn Mark**.

1. 9 Zeitungen, DM 18,–
2. 2 Pizzas, DM 16,–
3. 10 Briefmarken, DM 20,–
4. 3 Postkarten, DM 9,–
5. 3 Fragen, DM 0,–

Now think a little harder:

6. Was kostet eine Zeitung?
7. eine Pizza?
8. eine Briefmarke?
9. eine Postkarte?
10. eine Frage?

die Post	post office
die Buchhandlung	bookshop
das Fax	fax
senden	to send
wir	we
das Buch (die Bücher)	book
wo	where
auf der Post	at the post office
am besten	best
nehmen	to take

Wir (= we) is conjugated like *Sie:*

wir sind	we are
wir haben	we have
wir brauchen	we need
wir hören	we listen
wir arbeiten	we work
wir rufen … an	we call

The form ending in *-en* is also the infinitive, i.e. it also occurs with *können* etc.: *Ich kann heute nicht arbeiten* (= I can't work today).

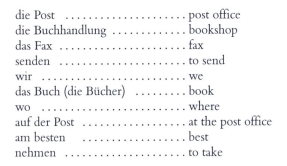

Entschuldigung.	Excuse me.
Einen Moment.	Just a moment.
Entschuldigung, bitte.	Excuse me, please.
Einen Moment.	Just a moment.
E-n-t-s-c-h-u-l-d-i-g-u-n-g.	E-x-c-u-s-e—m-e.
J-a-a-a-, bitte?	Y-e-e-e-s?
Haben Sie Briefmarken?	Do you have any stamps?
Hier ist nicht die Post!	This is not the post office!
Nein?	No?
Hier ist eine Buchhandlung.	This is a bookshop.
Aber ich brauche fünfzehn Briefmarken.	But I need fifteen stamps.
Tut mir Leid.	Sorry.
Können Sie ein Fax senden?	Can you send a fax?
Wir haben nur Bücher und Zeitungen.	We only have books and newspapers.
Wo bekomme ich die Briefmarken?	Where can I get the stamps?
Ja, auf der Post.	Well, at the post office.
Und wo ist die Post?	And where is the post office?
Am besten, Sie nehmen, ich weiß nicht.	You'd best take, I don't know.

Something's wrong here. The employee in the bookshop is in a bad mood, and to crown it all is being confused with someone in the post office.

Note: *ein* and *eine* have no plural, and the word concerned then simply has no article.

Singular:

Haben Sie eine Briefmarke?
Haben Sie ein Buch?
Haben Sie eine Zeitung?

Plural:

Haben Sie Briefmarke-n?
Haben Sie Büch-er?
Haben Sie Zeitung-en?

The little word *ja* doesn't mean "yes"; she's really saying "Well, what do you think?"

1. Find the right answer

1. Haben Sie Bücher?
2. Wo ist die Post?
3. Kann ich ein Fax senden?
4. Ist das alles?

5. Wo bekomme ich Postkarten?

a ■ Nein, nur auf der Post.
b ■ Auf der Post.
c ■ Ich weiß nicht.
d ■ Nein, hier ist keine Buchhandlung.
e ■ Nein, ich brauche auch Briefmarken.

2. Give some advice

*Am besten Sie nehmen **ein Taxi**.*

1. ein Taxi
2. eine Zeitung
3. einen Computer
4. ein Hotel
5. eine Briefmarke
6. einen Hamburger
7. ein Zimmer
8. eine Freundin
9. einen Student

3. Take away

*__Achtzehn__ minus **zwölf** ist **sechs**.*

1. 18 - 12 = _ _ _ _ _
2. 19 - 14 = _ _ _ _
3. 12 - 11 = _ _ _ _

4. 20 - 17 = _ _ _ _
5. 16 - 13 = _ _ _ _
6. 15 - 15 = _ _ _ _

4. Apologize

*Tut mir Leid, ich habe **kein Telefon**.*

1. das Telefon
2. die Telefonkarte
3. die Zeitung
4. die Briefmarke
5. das Buch
6. das Fax
7. der Brief

5. Fill in the gaps

1. Tut mir Leid, ich habe _ _ _ _ _ Bücher.
2. Vier und fünf, das macht _ _ _ _ Mark.
3. Am besten Sie _ _ _ _ _ _ ein Taxi.
4. Wo _ _ _ _ _ _ _ ich Briefmarken?
5. Kann ich ein Fax _ _ _ _ _ _ ?

Munich, Leopoldstraße, 5.30 on Thursday evening. Everything is at a complete standstill, with a four-lane traffic jam into town and a four-lane traffic jam out. A slim girl on a racing bike with a small rucksack on her back weaves her way between the cars. She's getting on fast, faster than the taxis or the buses, even though they have their own lane. Petra Günzler works for a courier service. In the age of the traffic jam, the bicycle has proved to be the fastest means of getting about.

The post office has got competition. It still usually manages to deliver a letter within Germany in one or two days, but its monopoly has been broken. Private parcel services operate throughout the country and, by the beginning of the new millenium, we will be able to choose who we give our letters to. At some point the yellow postboxes with the post horn will disappear. The posthorn incidentally is a throwback to the mail coachmen who ferried passengers and mail round the country more or less safely years ago. Our postal services started almost 500 years ago, when the Thurn and Taxis princes were given the hereditary office of postmaster general by the Emperor and built up a network of courier routes right across Europe from Vienna to Lisbon. From 1516 on private letters were carried, and in 1824 the first postboxes were set up in large towns.

The Thurn and Taxis family had to give up their postal monopoly in 1867. For a mere three million thalers compensation. Today they are again in the limelight – at least in the popular press.

From 20 to 100

20 *zwanzig*
30 *dreißig*
40 *vierzig*
50 *fünfzig*
60 *sechzig*
70 *siebzig*
80 *achtzig*
90 *neunzig*
100 *hundert*

The numbers from 20 to 100 are used by those in debt to say how many thousands of marks they've got to pay back. They are used by the rich to tell each other how many millions of marks they have stashed away in their accounts in the Bahamas.

Central Leipzig, in the last week of July. It's a quarter to nine and Eva Schwipper is waiting outside the doors of a large department store. When the doors open, dozens of women will storm the clothing department. In the summer sales *(Sommerschlussverkauf* or *SSV)* a great deal of stock is sold off cheaply. Those who have to count their pennies make their major purchases for the family then. Germany also has many poor people who cannot afford much and could not survive without help from the state. Even worse off are those who are ashamed of their hardship and hence do not claim the assistance they're entitled to. Eva Schwipper's husband has been unemployed for three years, and the two children want to keep up with their friends and have all the things currently considered "essential": computer games, jeans and jackets, trainers, rollerblades, school outings etc. The family has got into debt as a result. Half of all German households are in considerable debt, and the crisis always comes when there is not enough to pay the rent.

Two hours after Frau Schwipper, Helga Falk enters an elegant boutique nearby. She looks round for a quarter of an hour and chats with the shop assistant, tries on this and that, and then buys a suit and two skirts "just for the sake of it" for almost 2,200 DM, gets in her cabriolet and drives home. That is Germany too: so much money that people don't know what to do with it.

wünschen	to wish
das Brot	bread
das Weißbrot	white loaf
lieber	rather
das Vollkornbrot	wholemeal loaf
sonst noch was?	anything else?
die Butter	butter
wär's das?	is that all?
der Käse	cheese
das Gramm	gram
zusammen	altogether

The correct form of *Sonst noch was?* is *Sonst noch etwas? Etwas* also means "some" (see exercise B 5). Instead of the rather impolite question *Was?* (= What?) it is politer to ask *Wie bitte?* (= Pardon?)

500 grams = one pound (*Pfund*)
2 pounds = one kilogram
You will often hear, for example, *Ein dreiviertel Pfund Hackfleisch, bitte!* (= Three-quarters of a pound of mince, please). This is 375 grams.

Guten Tag, Sie wünschen?	Hello, can I help you?
Ein Brot bitte.	A loaf of bread, please.
Ich habe hier	
ein schönes Weißbrot.	I've got a nice white loaf here.
Nein, lieber ein Vollkornbrot. . . .	No, I'd rather have a wholemeal loaf.
Sonst noch was?	Anything else?
Butter bitte.	Some butter, please.
Wär's das?	Is that all?
Nein, ich brauche auch	
ein bisschen Käse.	No, I also need a bit of cheese.
Zweihundert Gramm?	Two hundred grams?
Ja, in Ordnung. Was macht das? . .	Yes, that's okay. How much is that?
Zwei zwanzig und fünf dreißig,	
sieben fünfzig und vier zwanzig,	
zusammen elf siebzig	Two twenty and five thirty, seven fifty and four twenty, that's eleven seventy altogether.

Ein schönes Weißbrot

Why is it *schön-es* here? This is where German gets complicated, with the finer details of declension. In this book, however, you don't need to learn the system of endings in its entirety. Here's something to help you: *das Brot, das* with an "s", *ein schöne-s Brot,* also with an "s". The "s" has to appear somewhere.
It's just something to keep in the back of your mind.

Germany probably has a larger selection of bread than any other country in the world. When Germans live abroad for a longer period, it is their dark wholemeal bread that they miss most.

Please don't take the easy way out and write figures. The author also had to type the words.

1. What's the missing number?

Zehn - zwanzig - dreißig - 1. _ _ _ _ _ _ _ - fünfzig -
2. _ _ _ _ _ _ _ - 3. _ _ _ _ _ _ _ - achtzig - 4. _ _ _ _ _ _ _ - hundert

+: *und* or *plus*
-: *weniger* or *minus*

If you can't get to grips with this exercise, maybe you've got a friend who's a maths teacher.

2. Find the right answer

1. $30 + 40 =$
   a ■ Dreißig und vierzig ist achtzig.
   b ■ Dreißig und vierzig ist siebzig.
2. $10 + 80 =$
   a ■ Zehn plus achtzig ist siebzig.
   b ■ Zehn plus achtzig ist neunzig.
3. $70 - 50 =$
   a ■ Siebzig minus fünfzig ist zwanzig.
   b ■ Siebzig und dreißig ist zwanzig.
4. $90 - 40 =$
   a ■ Neunzig minus vierzig ist sechzig.
   b ■ Neunzig minus vierzig ist fünfzig.

These are positive sentences.
In *7 zurück* comes right at the end, also in the question *Rufen Sie heute morgen aus Berlin zurück?*

3. Answer with "yes"

1/33

Ja, ich brauche ein Brot.
1. Brauchen Sie ein Brot?
2. Heißen Sie Mayer?
3. Kommen Sie morgen?
4. Sind Sie Fotografin?
5. Sprechen Sie ein bisschen Deutsch?
6. Wünschen Sie Butter?
7. Rufen Sie zurück?
8. Nehmen Sie Weißbrot?
9. Senden Sie ein Fax?

10. Answer 1. - 9. in the negative: *Nein, ich brauche kein Brot.*

Sentences like this are useful when you are talking about likes and dislikes. For example, when you're having a discussion about films: *Nein kein Robert Redford, lieber Robert de Niro.*

4. Say what you prefer

Nein, kein Weißbrot, lieber ein Vollkornbrot.
1. ein Weißbrot / ein Vollkornbrot
2. ein Brot / ein Käse
3. eine Zeitung / ein Buch
4. eine Postkarte / ein Brief
5. ein Brief / ein Fax

was darf es sein?	can I help you?
der Schinken	ham
mehr	more
weniger	less
die Wurst	sausage
die Salami	salami
geben	to give
mir	me
der Rotwein	red wine
vergessen	to forget

Was darf es sein? - an even politer alternative for *Sie wünschen?* (= Can I help you?)

You already know *mir* from the expression *tut mir Leid* (literally = does me pain).

Was darf es sein?	Can I help you?
Etwas Schinken bitte.	Some ham, please.
Wie viel, der Herr?	How much, sir?
So vierhundert Gramm.	Around four hundred grams.
Ein bisschen mehr?	Can it be a bit over?
Lieber ein bisschen weniger.	I'd rather have a bit less.
Sonst noch was?	Anything else?
Ja, ein bisschen Wurst.	Yes, a bit of sausage.
Hier habe ich eine schöne Salami.	I've got a nice salami here.
Geben Sie mir zweihundertfünfzig Gramm.	Give me two hundred and fifty grams.
Wär's das?	Is that all?
Ja, was macht das?	Yes, how much is that?
Dreizehn dreißig und vier – macht zusammen siebzehn dreißig.	Thirteen thirty and four is seventeen thirty altogether.
Oh, ich habe den Rotwein vergessen!	Oh, I've forgotten the red wine!

sein – the forms you already know:
ich bin   I am
Sie sind   you are

sein – some new forms:
er/sie ist   he/she is
wir sind   we are

There are a few letters missing here. Are you still learning the new vocabulary regularly? For example, saying the words out loud, then covering the German and saying the English, and a bit later covering the English and saying the German?

You can hear all these questions in a shop where you are still served. In the supermarket you get everything sealed in plastic. Sometimes there is still a proper cheese and cold cuts counter where you have to actually speak. Otherwise all you have to do is take your purchases to the check-out.

3 and 6 are perhaps a little difficult because two things go with white bread. But only one goes with red wine. Or have you ever eaten butter with red wine?

This sentence is also useful in other situations. For example when you are being pressurized to do something quickly. You will gain time if you say *Ich brauche noch ein bisschen Zeit* (= I need a bit more time).

This sentence is also useful elsewhere: *Geben Sie mir bitte noch etwas Zeit* (= Please give me a little more time).

1. What's missing?

1. das Voll _ _ _ _ brot
2. der Rot _ _ _ _
3. das Prob _ _ _
4. zurück _ _ _ _ _

5. die Buch _ _ _ _ lung
6. die Tel _ _ _ _ _ _ _ te
7. das _ eißbro _
8. int _ _ _ ssant

2. Which answer is right?

1. Brauchen Sie Brot?
   - a ■ Ja, Rotwein.
   - b ■ Nein, ich brauche Rotwein.
2. Darf's ein bisschen mehr sein?
   - a ■ Lieber mehr.
   - b ■ Kein Problem.
3. Sonst noch was?
   - a ■ Ich brauche auch Käse.
   - b ■ Ich habe auch Käse.
4. Guten Tag, Sie wünschen?
   - a ■ Kein Weißbrot.
   - b ■ Ein Vollkornbrot.

3. Find the partners

1. wissen
2. Brief
3. Rotwein
4. geben
5. tut mir Leid
6. Weißbrot
7. neugierig

a ■ Entschuldigung
b ■ Butter
c ■ Fax
d ■ interessant
e ■ verstehen
f ■ nehmen
g ■ Käse

4. What else do you need?

Ich brauche noch ein bisschen Käse.
1. Käse
2. Brot
3. Wurst
4. Butter
5. Wein
6. Salami

5. Ask politely for …

Geben Sie mir bitte etwas Brot.
1. Brot
2. Wurst
3. Butter
4. Salami
5. Käse
6. Wein

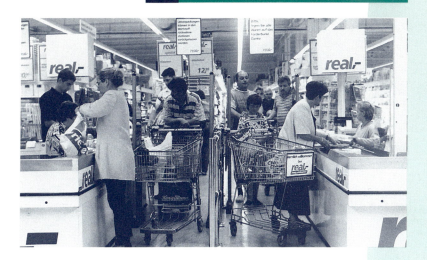

Shopping is anonymous and simple. Anonymous, because you get everything without having to say a word. And simple, because in the supermarket you pile everything you need into a shopping trolley, look at the till to see how much you have to pay, and then hand over the appropriate note and wait for the cashier to give you your change. Once upon a time there were a lot of little shops where you were served properly: *Gnädige Frau, darf es ein bisschen mehr sein, ich versichere Ihnen, unser Käse ist ganz vorzüglich. Hier bitte, wollen Sie so freundlich sein und einmal probieren?* (= Can it be a bit over, madam, I assure you our cheese is first class. May I offer you a piece to try?) Old people miss this kind of service, but we now live in the age of self-service. Today, if you want to buy groceries or clothes, you first need a car, since the best place to shop is in a mall or hypermarket and they are all out of town. Shopping expeditions have become a leisure activity in themselves. This sport is practised from a young age, and social scientists have discovered that adolescents do not spend most of their time on the football pitch or in front of the television, but in department stores.

Shopping is hardest for young mothers. In the shelves by the check-out, placed low down so they are visible to small children, are the most attractive sweets, and chocolate eggs with toys in them. While waiting in the queue, the child sees them and pesters until mummy gives in or screams "no". The poor child is not used to this and starts wailing with equal intensity. Being a consumer is sometimes hard work …

Corner shops

Once upon a time there was any number of little shops selling everything from sewing needles to bicycle bells, and from onions to salami. The supermarkets and hypermarkets have driven these friendly little establishments out of business, and gone are the days when you went into a shop for a chat. Bakers and butchers have remained, and greengrocers run by Turks and selling good fresh fruit and vegetables. Smaller villages usually now have no shop at all, and twice a week the delivery van drives in hooting loudly to announce its arrival.

To many people from other countries it looks as though the Germans earn an awful lot of money. But you have to remember that prices, and rents in particular, are very high.

People's ideas about what is most important in life have changed. There are yuppies who today loudly proclaim, *Geld ist die geilste Droge* (= Money is the greatest turn-on). No wonder we talk about a person being on a consumption high when his or her favourite expression is *Gehen wir einkaufen!* (= Let's go shopping), and every excursion to the shops results in a positive orgy of buying. *Ich zahle mit meiner Kreditkarte* (= I'll pay with my credit card) makes it all really easy.

The attractiveness of men and women is linked to what they wear, and the more they look like the nice, attractive young people in the adverts, the more successful they are considered to be. Adolescents have their own rules about what to wear, and teenage cliques are sometimes very cruel, rigorously excluding anyone not wearing trainers and jeans by the right designer. It is not always easy for parents, especially when one pair of trainers looks much like another, but it is the pair that costs not 50, but 185 marks that their offspring just has to have. Great importance is also attached to having the right clothing and equipment for any sport and leisure activity. Someone who does a bit of cycling gets kitted out as if taking part in the Tour de France, with special cycling trousers, sweatband, gloves with half fingers, tinted dazzle-free glasses and of course a little computer on the handlebars to measure personal performance.

In the land of poets and philosophers, Formula-I drivers and footballers have become the dominant role models.

das Geschenk .... present
gehen wir .... let's go
einkaufen .... shopping, to shop
das Geld .... money
mit .... with
die Kreditkarte .... credit card
zahlen .... to pay
die D-Mark .... (German) mark
wechseln .... to change
die Bank .... bank

Back-to-front numbers

21 *einundzwanzig*
22 *zweiundzwanzig*
23 *dreiundzwanzig*
24 *vierundzwanzig*
25 *fünfundzwanzig*
26 *sechsundzwanzig*
27 *siebenundzwanzig*
28 *achtundzwanzig*
29 *neunundzwanzig*
30 *dreißig*

It won't have escaped your notice: *sieb-zehn* – first the units, then the tens. This applies not just from 13 to 19, as in English, but right through to 99.

Ich habe etwas vergessen. ...... I've forgotten something.
Ja, was? .... Yes, what (have you forgotten)?
Ich brauche ein Geschenk. ..... I need a present.
Gehen wir einkaufen. .... Let's go shopping.
Ja, aber ich habe ein Problem. ... Yes, but I have a problem.
So? .... Oh really?
Ja, ich habe kein Geld. .... Yes, I don't have any money.
Ich kann mit meiner
Kreditkarte zahlen. .... I can pay with my credit card.
Ich habe Geld,
aber keine D-Mark. .... I've got money, but no marks.
Gehen wir Geld wechseln. ..... Let's go and change
                                some money.
Gut, wo ist hier eine Bank? ..... Good, where is there a bank
                                round here?

1. Suggestions beginning with "Let's go…"

1/38

All you do is follow Gehen wir … with a verb and the sentence is complete. It sounds friendlier to make a suggestion like this than to give a command: Kaufen Sie ein!

*Gehen wir **einkaufen**.*

1. einkaufen
2. ein Fax senden
3. arbeiten
4. Geld wechseln
5. mit Maria sprechen
6. alles zahlen
7. Peter anrufen

2. Say "no": *kein or kein-e?*

1/39

Don't forget: der and das are definite articles, while the indefinite article is ein, from which we get kein; die is definite, eine, from which we get kein-e, is indefinite.

*Nein, ich **habe kein Geld**.*

1. Haben Sie Geld?
2. Haben Sie Butter?
3. Sind Sie Journalist?
4. Haben Sie ein Problem?
5. Kaufen Sie ein Geschenk?
6. Brauchen Sie Geld?
7. Hören Sie Radio?

3. Translate into German

Translations are unfortunately important, and they are difficult when you don't know some of the words and have to paraphrase them: "we're going to Hamburg with a long thing that runs on two rails."

1. Sorry, I don't have any money. _____
2. Let's go and change some money. _____
3. I need stamps. _____
4. I am buying cheese and ham. _____
5. Give me some red wine. _____
6. You are curious. _____
7. I am paying by credit card. _____

4. What have you forgotten?

Vergessen means: 1. "forget" and 2. "forgotten". If it appears with haben, it means "forgotten" and refers to the past. But we'll save that for later.

*Ich habe **die Zeitung** vergessen.*

1. die Zeitung
2. das Geschenk
3. den Student
4. das Buch
5. die Frage
6. meine Frau

5. What is the missing verb?

This exercise is designed to fix some of the verbs in your mind. Can you fill all the gaps without looking anything up?

1. Kann ich hier mit Dollar _ _ _ _ _ _ ?
2. Wir gehen am besten Geld _ _ _ _ _ _ _ .
3. Ich gehe ein Geschenk _ _ _ _ _ _ .
4. Gehen wir ein Fax _ _ _ _ _ _ .

möchte	would like
der Reisescheck	traveller's cheque
oder	or
in bar	(in) cash
der Kurs	exchange rate
heute	today
probieren	to try
andere	other
die Bank	bank
jetzt	now
die Kommission	commission

The *Kurs* is sometimes also called *Wechselkurs*, *Wechsel* being the word for "exchange". Compound words always function in the same way: the second part gives the general meaning *(Scheck)*, while the first describes it more precisely *(Reise* = Travel): *Reisescheck*.

The pound sterling is called *Pfund* in German, just like the word for a pound (weight).

Sie wünschen?	Can I help you?
Ich möchte 200 Dollar wechseln.	I would like to change 200 dollars.
In Reisechecks oder in bar?	In traveller's cheques or cash?
In bar. Wie ist der Kurs heute?	Cash. What's the exchange rate today?
Ein Dollar – eins dreiundfünfzig siebzehn.	One dollar is one fifty-three seventeen.
Das ist aber nicht gut!	That's not very good!
Probieren Sie es auf einer anderen Bank.	Try another bank.
Nein, nein, ich brauche das Geld jetzt.	No, no, I need the money now.
Hier sind zweihunderteinund-neunzig vierunddreißig.	That's two hundred and ninety-one, thirty-four.
So wenig?	So little?
Wir nehmen fünfzehn Mark Kommission.	We take fifteen marks commission.
Ohh- ohh- ooh...	Ohh- ohh- ooh...

Learning tip

You can also use the page numbers in this book to learn your numbers. Just look at the figures, say the number out loud and then look at the word next to it to see if you were right. This is a good thing to do when you're in the underground or on a plane or when there's nothing worthwhile on TV.

Kurs can also mean "course" (i.e. lessons) or "class".
So in this dialogue means the same as it does in English.

1. Find the right answer

1. Wie ist der Kurs heute?
   - a ■ Ich brauche das Geld jetzt.
   - b ■ Ich glaube zwei dreizehn neunzig.

2. Sie geben aber wenig.
   - a ■ Wir nehmen keine Kommission.
   - b ■ Wir nehmen Kommission.

3. Können Sie Dollar wechseln?
   - a ■ Tut mit Leid, nur Reiseschecks.
   - b ■ Wir verkaufen Dollar.

4. Brauchen Sie das Geld jetzt?
   - a ■ Morgen ist auch Okay.
   - b ■ Ich brauche das Geld morgen nicht.

2. Sort into matching pairs

1. 69
2. 48
3. 96
4. 84

a sechsundneunzig
b vierundachtzig
c achtundvierzig
d neunundsechzig

3. Say what you want

*Ich möchte **ein Buch kaufen**.*

1. ein Buch kaufen
2. das verstehen
3. Michael Jackson heißen
4. Ingenieur sein
5. ein Geschenk bekommen
6. 200 Dollar wechseln
7. morgen alleine kommen
8. am Computer arbeiten
9. mit Kreditkarte zahlen
10. einkaufen gehen

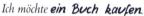

1/41

4. Write out and read these numbers

zwölf

1. 12
2. 23
3. 34
4. 45
5. 56
6. 67
7. 78
8. 89

Anyone who goes to Frankfurt every three or four months will be taken by surprise time and again. Every time there seems to be another skyscraper in the city, with each new addition higher than the previous one. Because of its architecture, Frankfurt am Main is also known colloquially as *Mainhattan.* This is where the big money is in Germany. The *Bundesbank* was established here after the Second World War, and the bank was soon followed by the stock market, which now handles 80 % of all stocks and shares in Germany. Money, they say, is like a magnet, so other banks were also attracted to the metropolis on the Main. Today all the major banks in the world are represented here, and Frankfurt's location in the middle of Europe has proved very convenient.

Every autumn the city hosts the International Book Fair, the largest fair of its kind. Publishing houses and authors from all over the world gather here, and there is always an interesting main theme.

The city of Frankfurt also has a remarkable "mile of museums" and is a good example of an important centre that has been established in a federal republic outside the capital. Another interesting fact is that around 30 % of Frankfurt's population consists of foreigners, living in relative harmony with the Germans.

And of course, we mustn't forget to mention Frankfurt's most famous son, the poet and playwright Johann Wolfgang von Goethe, Germany's "Shakespeare".

**Frankfurt:
facts and figures**

- The Frankfurt Paulskirche: for the whole of 1848 this church was used for the sessions of the first democratic parliament.
- The largest station in Europe. 1,500 trains a day (including the S-Bahn, the suburban rail network)
- The largest volume of air freight in Europe
- The second highest number of passengers after London
- The first complete edition of Goethe's works comprised 143 volumes.
- The largest book fair in the world
- The highest buildings in Germany

Here we want to see whether you have read the texts about Germany carefully. Of course you are not expected to take all the questions seriously. Perhaps some of the answers will amuse you …

1. Which is right?

1. Self-important people with mobile phones are irritating
   a ■ in their jet.
   b ■ in the cinema.
   c ■ in the forest.
2. The trainers every teenager must have cost
   a ■ as much as a small car.
   b ■ so much that mother is cross at having to pay for them.
   c ■ next to nothing.
3. The Thurn und Taxis princes
   a ■ invented the taxi.
   b ■ invented the bicycle.
   c ■ founded the postal service.
4. Adolescents spend most of their leisure time
   a ■ on the football field.
   b ■ in department stores looking for things to buy.
   c ■ in front of the television in their parents' living room.
5. Chocolate eggs with toys in them
   a ■ are put near the till in supermarkets.
   b ■ are forbidden in kindergartens.
   c ■ are not accepted as presents.
6. The metropolis of Frankfurt is associated with
   a ■ the Brandenburger Tor.
   b ■ the Oktoberfest.
   c ■ Goethe and the Deutsche Bank.

2. Answers and questions

Tut mir Leid is a polite way of saying no.

1. Kann ich Sie anrufen.
2. Kann ich hier Postkarten bekommen?
3. Wünschen Sie ein Weißbrot?
4. Darf es ein bisschen mehr sein?
5. Bezahlen Sie in bar?
6. Brauchen Sie das Geld morgen?

a ■ Tut mir Leid, ich brauche das Geld jetzt.
b ■ Tut mir Leid, ich habe nur eine Kreditkarte.
c ■ Tut mir Leid, lieber ein bisschen weniger.
d ■ Tut mir Leid, lieber ein Vollkornbrot.
e ■ Tut mir Leid, wir sind eine Buchhandlung.
f ■ Tut mir Leid, ich habe kein Telefon.

3. Multiple choice

Be careful, some of the wrong answers are possible, but sound very odd. What we are of course looking for are the most obvious solutions.

1. Können Sie Dollars _____?
   a ■ kaufen
   b ■ senden
   c ■ wechseln
2. Ich möchte mit _____ zahlen.
   a ■ Kommission
   b ■ Geschenk
   c ■ Kreditkarte
3. Ich brauche ein _____ Käse.
   a ■ sprechen
   b ■ bisschen
   c ■ geben
4. Was _____ das zusammen?
   a ■ macht
   b ■ möchte
   c ■ zahle
5. Haben Sie _____ und Briefmarken?
   a ■ Buchhandlung
   b ■ Postkarten
   c ■ Zimmer
6. Kein Problem, wir rufen _____.
   a ■ zurück
   b ■ morgen
   c ■ in bar

4. Sense and nonsense

There is no doubt that children learn languages the simplest way – without thinking. They prefer to play, and we want to do that too, play with the words a little, as even nonsense is sometimes rather creative, wouldn't you agree?

1. I would like a wholemeal loaf with excuse me.
2. Do you need 200 grams of traveller's cheques?
3. Let's go and live credit cards.
4. Will you take white bread or computers?
5. The problem is wonderful.
6. Do you speak red wine?

Nowadays it is not only musicians you find busking in pedestrian precincts. There is a wide range of entertainment, especially in summer, from fire-eaters to mime artists. They're always quickly surrounded by a crowd, although sometimes unwary passers-by can find themselves becoming part of the action.

Mr Muller has a few days to spare and wants to see something of Germany. He goes to Osnabrück, where he has an old friend. They have arranged to meet near the station in the afternoon on the day after he arrives. Mr Muller still has some time before their meeting and just walks through the town to "get the feel of it". The pedestrian precinct in the centre is very pleasant, you don't have to look out for cars, and it is quite quiet. Yesterday evening Mr Muller came here too; there was an oppressive stillness. When the streets are deserted, the town seems totally lifeless. In the business districts there's nothing going on at all after the shops close. Only a few people live here, and the only social life is confined to the bars and restaurants. In the daytime, however, the pedestrian precinct is very lively with displays and stands set up along it, hurrying people and a Russian street musician playing melancholy tunes on his accordion. Perhaps he's playing sad songs because so few people are stopping to listen, and thinks maybe a bit of sympathy would induce them to part with a coin or a small note.

It's time for our Mr Muller's meeting, but he's got lost. He asks, *Wo ist der Bahnhof, bitte?* (= Where is the station, please?) The passer-by, who looks as if she's been living here for at least 75 years, says, *Oh, das ist ganz einfach* (= Oh, that's very easy).

When you know your way around it's always easy ...

der Bahnhof	....	station
einfach	....	easy
immer	....	always
geradeaus	....	straight on
rechts	....	right
dann	....	then
zweite	....	second
die Straße	....	road, street
links	....	left
schwierig	....	difficult

Opposites

rechts	right
links	left
einfach	easy
schwierig	difficult

Entschuldigung ...	....	Excuse me ...
Ja bitte?	....	Yes?
Ich habe eine Frage.	....	I have a question.
Ja?	....	Yes?
Wo ist der Bahnhof, bitte?	......	Where's the station, please?
Oh, das ist sehr einfach.	....	Oh, that's very easy.
Aha ...	....	Ahh ...
Hier immer geradeaus.	....	Straight on along here.
Ja ...	....	Yes ...
An der Post rechts.	....	Right at the post office.
Ja ...	....	Yes ...
Dann die zweite Straße links.	...	Then the second road on the left.
Ja ...	....	Yes ...
Dann rechts.	....	Then right.
Ja ...	....	Yes ...
Und dann fragen Sie wieder.	....	And then ask again.
Sehr schwierig.	....	Very difficult.

Ordinal numbers 1–10

erste	first
zwei-te	second
dritte	third
vier-te	fourth
fünf-te	fifth
sechs-te	sixth
sieb-te	seventh
ach-te	eighth
neun-te	ninth
zehn-te	tenth

Now you know all the ordinal numbers – provided of course you have already learnt the normal numbers. Note: *siebte* not *siebente*

1. Translate into German

The best thing to do is learn the new words, then you don't need to turn back to the previous page.

1. straight ahead _____
2. very difficult _____
3. the station _____
4. second street on the left _____
5. Ask again! _____

2. Which question is right?

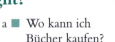

Too much routine is not a good thing. We have simply turned this exercise round and this time are asking for the right question. If the exercise is too fast on the cassette/CD, use the pause button.

1. An der Post links ist eine Buchhandlung.
   a ■ Wo kann ich Bücher kaufen?
   b ■ Haben Sie Briefmarken?

2. Fünfzig Mark.
   a ■ Was macht das zusammen?
   b ■ Können Sie Geld wechseln?

3. Die zweite Straße links.
   a ■ Wo ist die Post?
   b ■ Wie viele Straßen hat Salzburg?

4. Ja, morgen bitte um neun Uhr.
   a ■ Haben Sie ein Telefon?
   b ■ Kann ich Sie anrufen?

3. Ordinal numbers

You only need to remember *erste* and *dritte,* since all the other ordinal numbers are regular, i.e. a *-te* is added to the cardinal number.

1. Helmut Kohl ist der (6.) _ _ _ _ _ _ _ Bundeskanzler von Deutschland.
2. Meine (2.) _ _ _ _ _ _ Frau heißt Maria.
3. Ich habe noch eine (3.) _ _ _ _ _ _ Frage.
4. Papst Johannes der (23.) _ _ _ _ _ _ _ _ _ _ _ _ _ _ _ _ _ _ .

4. Find the opposites

Put the words into pairs of opposites.

1. alleine	2. weniger	3. links
4. kommen	5. schwierig	6. nehmen
7. ja	8. Käse	9. gut
10. Herr		

a Wurst	b nein	c geben
d einfach	e gehen	f rechts
g mehr	h zusammen	i Frau
j schlimm		

der Urlaub . . . . holiday
müde . . . . tired
viel . . . . a lot, hard
gearbeitet . . . . worked
wegfahren . . . . to go away
wohin? . . . . where to?
nach . . . . to
bleiben . . . . to stay
das Reisebüro . . . . travel agency
die Idee . . . . idea

There's nothing for it, the words just have to be learned! Of course it doesn't matter if you forget a word now and again. There will be some you just can't get into your head. Don't let it worry you!

Past:
haben + gearbeitet

ge-arbeit-et is the past participle.
The following participles are formed in the same way:

glauben	*ge-glaub-t*
hören	*ge-hör-t*
kaufen	*ge-kauf-t*
leben	*ge-leb-t*
machen	*ge-mach-t*
senden	*ge-send-et*
wechseln	*ge-wechsel-t*
zahlen	*ge-zahl-t*

Ich brauche Urlaub! . . . . I need a holiday!
Sind Sie müde? . . . . Are you tired?
Ja, ich habe viel gearbeitet. . . . . . Yes, I've been working hard.
Dann müssen Sie wegfahren. . . . Then you must go away.
Wohin? Das ist die Frage. . . . . . . Where to? That's the question.
Vielleicht nach Spanien? . . . . Maybe to Spain?
Nein, das möchte ich nicht. . . . . . No, I wouldn't like that.
Nach Frankreich? . . . . To France?
Das möchte ich auch nicht. . . . . . I wouldn't like that either.
Bleiben Sie hier. . . . . Stay here.
Nein, wirklich nicht! . . . . No, certainly not!
Dann müssen Sie
ins Reisebüro gehen. . . . . Then you must go
to a travel agency.
Ja, das ist eine gute Idee. . . . . . . Yes, that's a good idea.

1. *Ich habe …*
2. *heute sehr viel …*
3. *gearbeitet*
The past participle comes right at the end.

A German peculiarity: inversion

Dann müssen Sie …
If a sentence does not begin with the person that is the subject, then it goes like this:
1. Beginning
   (Dann, Vielleicht)
2. Verb
   (müssen, gehen)
3. Person/Subject
   (ich, Sie, Herr X)

1. How does the sentence continue?

All these sentences are in the past. Your job is to find the word to complete them so that they make sense, and at the same time take note of how the past is formed.

1. Wir haben das nicht
2. Ich habe ein Auto
3. Haben Sie das Fax
4. Er hat in Basel
5. Haben Sie die Dollars

a ■ gesendet?
b ■ geglaubt.
c ■ gekauft.
d ■ gewechselt?
e ■ gelebt.

2. Which answer is right?

In this exercise look and see if the response has been properly constructed – if it does not start with the subject, then the verb must come second and the subject third.

1. Ich möchte wegfahren.

a ■ Dann müssen Sie ins Reisebüro.
b ■ Dann Sie müssen ins Reisebüro.

2. Kann ich Sie anrufen?

a ■ Vielleicht Sie rufen morgen an.
b ■ Vielleicht rufen Sie morgen an.

3. Wo ist der Bahnhof?

a ■ Das ich weiß nicht.
b ■ Das weiß ich nicht.

4. Fahren Sie in Urlaub?

a ■ Morgen ich fahre nach Tirol.
b ■ Morgen fahre ich nach Tirol.

5. Kann ich jetzt kommen?

a ■ Um neun Sie können kommen.
b ■ Um neun können Sie kommen.

3. Fill in the gaps

Here the missing word is given at the end of the sentence in English.

1. Das ist eine gute _ _ _ _. (idea)
2. Gehen Sie am besten in ein _ _ _ _ _ _ _ _ _. (travel agency)
3. Fahren Sie _ _ _ _ Amerika? (to)
4. Die _ _ _ _ _ _ Straße links. (third)
5. Jetzt können Sie keinen _ _ _ _ _ _ machen. (holiday)
6. Diese Frage ist sehr _ _ _ _ _ _ _ _ _. (difficult)

4. Put in the past tense

Proceed as follows:
1. What is the verb?
2. Put a *habe* in place of the verb.
3. Add the participle at the end, i.e. *ge-* plus the root of the verb plus the ending *-t*.

*Ich habe **ein Buch** gekauft.*

1. Ich kaufe ein Buch.
2. Ich glaube das nicht.
3. Ich lebe in Berlin.
4. Ich wechsle zwanzig D-Mark.
5. Ich zahle mit der Kreditkarte.
6. Ich mache Urlaub.

Half the families in the Federal Republic have two cars – it's no wonder that the whole society is suffering from what might be called mobility mania. Those who suffer most are the commuters who live out in the country. They may have to drive 75 km (47 miles) to work and 75 km home again afterwards. And it's the same thing every day: traffic jams going into town in the morning, and traffic jams going out of town in the evening.

In the evenings when offices shut and shops are still open, the town centres are full to bursting. Everyone has something they need to buy on their way home, no-one can find a parking place and, because there are so many cars, they only get through the traffic lights three at a time. Being a consumer becomes stress.

When people take a holiday, they rarely do the one thing that would be relaxing: put their feet up and ignore the rest of the world. No, they've got to go away. Any place that can be reached in a day or two they drive to in their own car. Thus on certain days in the summer holidays there are jams over a hundred kilometres long on the autobahns.

Travel to distant places has also become fashionable. Travelling is a status symbol, it looks good if you can send a postcard to your colleagues from the Maldives or the South Pacific. Environmentalists complain about the air traffic, and the car industry is still reluctant to produce cars that only use three litres: mobility mania isn't exactly designed to solve the ecological problems of our planet.

Summer holidays

If all the Germans, Austrians and Swiss were to go on holiday at the same time, it would be total chaos. Within Germany a solution has been found to this problem: the *Länder* stagger their six-week school summer holiday with starting dates between the middle of June and the beginning of August.

Many people have had enough of traffic problems and have taken to cycling. Workers, teachers, members of parliament – all those who don't live too far away from their work – cycle there and back every day. Most towns now have a comprehensive network of asphalt cycle tracks.

Special rate tickets

When you go by train you can generally find something cheaper than the normal ticket: there are weekend tickets for small groups, there is the *BahnCard* which offers a 50 % reduction for the whole year, and there are special rates for schoolchildren, students, pensioners etc. Information can be obtained from most travel agents or at station ticket offices.

Isolde Schaub is sitting in the ICE, the Intercity Express, from Munich to Frankfurt. After the train has left Stuttgart she looks at her watch, then out of the window, then at her watch again and says to her neighbour, "My God this train is slow! I have to be in Frankfurt in ten minutes." At that precise moment a pleasant woman's voice is heard over the loudspeaker announcing, "Ladies and gentlemen, our current speed is 250 km (153 miles) per hour." Speed is relative, and Isolde Schaub is not going to be in Frankfurt, another 150 km (93 miles) away, in ten minutes. We live in the age of superlatives, and everything must always be faster, higher or more beautiful, otherwise no-one is interested.

The Deutsche Bahn, the German Railways, are doing everything they can to make things convenient for travellers, and the large cities of Germany in fact have an hourly service between them. The trains are faster than fast cars on the autobahn – they're constantly being held up by overtaking lorries, roadworks and traffic jams.

But travelling by train with a normal ticket is far from cheap.

die Fahrkarte	ticket
fahren	to go, to travel
die Klasse	class
kommt drauf an	that depends
voll	full
wann	when
der ICE	Intercity Express
um zwölf Uhr zwanzig	at twelve twenty
ab	from ... on
die Platz-Reservierung	seat reservation

**kommt drauf an –
that depends**

Whenever you want to gain
a little time or don't want
to commit yourself, when
the question seems too
simple or when you don't
want to give an answer,
then *kommt drauf an* is a
useful expression.

Eine Fahrkarte nach München bitte.	A ticket to Munich, please.
Fahren Sie erster oder zweiter Klasse?	Do you want to go first or second class?
Kommt drauf an.	That depends.
Wie? Kommt drauf an?	What? It depends?
Ist der Zug voll?	Is the train full?
Wann fahren Sie?	When are you travelling?
Mit dem ICE um zwölf Uhr zwanzig.	With the Intercity Express at twelve twenty.
Der ist nicht voll, vielleicht ab Mannheim.	That's not full, perhaps from Mannheim on.
Dann bitte zweiter Klasse.	Then second class, please.
Möchten Sie eine Platz-Reservierung?	Would you like a seat reservation?
Ja, bitte.	Yes, please.
Macht zusammen DM 112,80. ..	That's 112 marks 80 altogether.
Kann ich mit Scheck bezahlen? ..	Can I pay by cheque?
Kein Problem.	No problem.

ICE, short for Intercity
Express, is the fastest train
in Germany, looks very
futuristic and has a compe-
titor in France: the TGV. The
next generation of trains is
already waiting in the
wings: the magnetic
cushion train, which is said
to be able to go up to
500 km (310 miles) per
hour. But it's very expensive
to develop, and there is
already a gaping hole in
the state coffers. It will be a
few years yet before we
can go from Hamburg to
Berlin in under an hour.

Important words to know:
die Auskunft information
die Abfahrt departure
die Ankunft arrival
das Gleis track
der Bahnsteig platform

1. When does the train leave?

Um **sechs Uhr fünfzehn**.

1. 6:15   2. 14:23   3. 0:44
4. 7:30   5. 10:16   6. 21:22
7. 5:43   8. 19:59   9. 12:10

2. Find the right answer

1. Wohin fahren Sie?   a ■ Ich komme aus Dortmund.
                                   b ■ Ich fahre nach Dortmund.

2. Möchten Sie eine Platzreservierung?
                                   a ■ Ich habe keine Reservierung.
                                   b ■ Nein, brauche ich nicht.

3. Fahren Sie mit dem Zug?   a ■ Ja, mit dem ICE.
                                   b ■ Ja, wir fahren mit dem Auto.

4. Wann möchten Sie fahren?   a ■ Vielleicht um zehn Uhr elf.
                                   b ■ Ich habe keine Fahrkarte.

3. Ask questions

Ist **der Zug voll?**

1. Zug, voll   5. Zimmer, schön
2. Idee, gut   6. Student, verheiratet
3. Journalist, neugierig   7. Dollar-Kurs, interessant
4. Doktor, krank   8. Problem, schwierig

4. Find the partners

1. Das ist kein   a ■ Frage.
2. Ich habe eine einfache   b ■ zweiter Klasse.
3. Ich brauche ein   c ■ gute Idee.
4. Das ist eine   d ■ schwieriges Problem.
5. Ich fahre immer nur   e ■ schönes Geschenk für Maria.

einchecken	to check in
welche	which
die Fluglinie	airline
das Ticket	ticket
verdammt	damn
die Maschine	plane
die Minute	minute
das Gepäck	luggage
direkt	straight, direct
der Ausgang	exit

Verdammt – this is a swearword. There are occasions in life when you just have to swear. *Verdammt* is always appropriate when you run to the station to see the train pulling out, or when you flunk an exam.

Maschine is a general word which is also used for "plane". Otherwise the plane is *das Flugzeug* or in modern day-to-day speech *der Flieger*.

You can see that the train is the traditional means of transport and the plane the modern one from the language. Compare:

am Bahnhof

die Fahrkarte ticket
die Auskunft information
die Abfahrt departure
(*fahren* – to go, travel, drive)
der Bahnsteig platform

am Flughafen

das Ticket ticket
die Information information
der Abflug departure
der Flug flight
(*fliegen* – to fly)
Gate gate

Kann ich hier einchecken?	Can I check in here?
Welche Fluglinie?	Which airline?
Lufthansa.	Lufthansa.
Okay. Ihr Ticket bitte.	Okay. Your ticket, please.
Bitte schön.	Here you are.
Oh, verdammt	Oh, damn ...
Haben Sie ein Problem?	Is there a problem?
Nein, ja, der Computer geht nicht.	No, yes, the computer's not working.
Ja, aber ... meine Maschine geht in dreißig Minuten.	Yes, but ... my plane leaves in thirty minutes.
Tut mir Leid.	Sorry.
Und mein Gepäck?	And my luggage?
Am besten Sie gehen	You'd best go ...
Wohin?	Where?
... direkt zu Ausgang fünfundvierzig.	straight to exit forty-five.

Form proper sentences or questions – you only need to rearrange the words.

1. Put in the correct order

1. Maschine - Die - in - geht - 15 - Minuten _____
2. Sie - zweiter - Klasse?- Fahren _____
3. Zug - voll - nicht - sehr - ist - Der _____
4. Sie - Reservierung? - eine - Möchten _____
5. einchecken? - Kann - ich - hier _____

Child's play for all those who've learnt their words. For the others it's a test. Geniuses of course never have to learn vocabulary, but they are rare beings.

2. What is it in English?

1. das Gepäck _____
2. kommt drauf an _____
3. die Maschine _____
4. der Ausgang _____
5. die Fahrkarte _____
6. verdammt _____
7. welche _____
8. fahren _____
9. der Zug _____
10. voll _____

Um (= at) is used to give the exact time. We are learning first the formal language of any timetable information service, and will later learn what normal people actually say.

3. At what time?

Um *vier Uhr fünfunddreißig.*
1. 04:35
2. 15:46
3. 23:57
4. 01:16
5. 09:33
6. 13:05
7. 17:18
8. 19:45

Simply put the sentences in the past. To remind you: the past is formed with the appropriate form of *haben* and the past participle, which is constructed by putting a *ge-* in front of the root of the verb and a *-t* at the end of it. Sentence 2 is an exception: here the infinitive and the past participle are the same: with no *ge-* in front and with *-en* at the end.

4. Put in the past tense

Sie *haben Rotwein gekauft.*
1. Sie kaufen Rotwein.
2. Sie vergessen die Frage.
3. Sie arbeiten sehr viel.
4. Sie leben in Frankreich.
5. Sie hören nicht.
6. Sie brauchen Geld.

Of course other words will always fit in here as well. For example *Kann ich hier meine Probleme mit einer Flasche Rotwein vergessen?* (= Can I forget my problems here with a bottle of red wine?) But the solutions are key words from this unit, and the number of letters is also indicated.

5. What's missing?

1. Kann ich hier _ _ _ _ _ _ _ _ _?
2. Fahren Sie zweiter _ _ _ _ _ _?
3. Meine _ _ _ _ _ _ _ _ geht in fünfzehn Minuten.
4. Der _ _ _ ist nicht sehr voll.
5. Mein Zug geht in zehn _ _ _ _ _ _ _.

Flying is a controversial means of travel, and environmentalists complain that the air pollution per passenger and kilometre is much greater than that caused by trains or buses. But Germany is not a large country, and an air ticket is almost twice as expensive as a train ticket.

It is almost only business people who fly within Germany: they have little time and their ticket is paid for them. People generally use planes for long trips, since for shorter trips the Intercity Express is faster. Airports are always outside city centres. You first have to get from the centre to the airport to check in your luggage half an hour before the flight, then you have to wait, then there is the flight and at the end of it another wait for the luggage. Then you take an expensive taxi or a bus that perhaps only goes every half an hour to the centre.

When you arrive late at the airport and don't know which counter to go to it can get stressful. *Kann ich hier einchecken?* (= Can I check in here) – this question is not always answered with *ja*. If the nice airline employee then says, *Tut mir Leid der Computer geht nicht* (= Sorry, the computer's not working), your blood pressure will go up a bit more.

Children flying alone are also a common sight. In a society where one in three marriages ends in divorce, it's not uncommon to find the father moving, for example, from Hamburg to Munich, 800 kilometres away, leaving mother and child behind. Every fortnight the child makes the trip to Munich – provided of course the parents can afford it.

The most important airlines

Germany

*Lufthansa
Condor
LTU
Aero Lloyd
Hapag Lloyd*

Switzerland

Swissair

Austria

*Austrian Airlines
Lauda Air*

How do I find a taxi?

Tell hotel reception, and they'll order you one.

There are taxis waiting round the clock at the airport and – at least in large towns – outside the station.

In the telephone book they are listed under *Taxi* or *Taxen* – that's the plural. Ring the number and in three minutes they'll be at your door.

In many towns there's a somewhat cheaper alternative which is called *City-Car* or something similar. These are usually slightly smaller cars.

I am in Bern, Salzburg or Wiesbaden. It is already quite late, and at night no respectable person is supposed to be abroad. The last bus often leaves before midnight. There is nothing for it but to take a taxi.

I have an important appointment in a strange town and arrive by train. There's very little time before the meeting is due to begin, I don't know the bus routes and it's too far to walk. There's nothing for it but to take a taxi.

I'm invited to a party or a dinner. The host likes good wine and proudly uncorks one bottle after the other, each one delicious. If I'm wise I will have anticipated this beforehand and not come by car. If not, then it's better if I leave my car where it is. The police are particularly fond of stopping you at night and having you blow in the little bag: "Let's see how much he's drunk." There's nothing for it but to take a taxi.

Taxis don't cruise through the city until summoned by someone by the roadside. They are at special taxi stands: at the station, in front of the theatre, at the underground. *Gibt es hier Taxis?* (= Are there any taxis around here?) is the question to ask when you need a taxi. At the end of the trip the answer to the question *Was schulde ich Ihnen?* (= How much do I owe you?) may come as an unpleasant surprise: nowhere are taxis as expensive as they are in Germany.

es gibt	there is/are
das Taxi	taxi
nee	no
unbedingt	really
dort drüben	over there
das Hotel	hotel
zum ersten Mal	for the first time
reden	to talk
schulden	to owe
Ihnen	(to) you

es gibt – When you are inquiring about the existence of something, *es gibt* can always be used. *Gibt es ein Hotel hier? Gibt es ein Telefon?* Anyone who's short of cash can for example ask, *Gibt es eine Spielbank hier?* (= Is there a casino here?)

unbedingt – This word always sounds very important.

Gibt es hier Taxis?	Are there any taxis around here?
Nee.	No.
Ich brauche unbedingt ein Taxi.	I really must find a taxi.
Dort drüben ist ein Telefon.	There's a telephone over there.
Ah, ja.	Oh, yes.
Am besten Sie rufen ein Taxi. . . .	You'd best call for a taxi.
Danke schön.	Thank you very much.

hier where the speaker is
dort at some distance from the speaker

drüben means on the other side of the road, of the country, the ocean … as seen from here.

Zum Hotel Walhalla bitte.	The Hotel Walhalla please.
Okay. Sind Sie nicht aus Osnabrück?	You're not from Osnabrück, are you?
Nein.	No.
Sind Sie zum ersten Mal hier? . . .	Are you here for the first time?
Nein.	No.
Möchten Sie nicht reden?	Do you not want to talk?
Nein …	No…
… Hier sind wir.	Here we are.
Was schulde ich Ihnen?	How much do I owe you?
Macht vierzehn Mark zwanzig.	That's fourteen marks twenty.
Hier haben Sie fünfzehn Mark.	Here are fifteen marks.

reden is a little more than *sprechen*, with *reden* the content is also implied. *Sprechen* is more the actual process of speaking.

Was schulde ich Ihnen ? – this question is always right when you are asking how much you have to pay, in a taxi, a pub …

1. Doing something for the first time

*Ich **bin** zum ersten Mal **in** Osnabrück.*

1. in Osnabrück sein
2. mit dem ICE fahren
3. am Computer arbeiten
4. ein Fax senden
5. das verstehen

6. ein Flugzeug kaufen
7. mit Kreditkarte zahlen
8. nach Berlin kommen
9. Maria anrufen

2. Which answer is right?

1. Taxi! Zum Hotel Europa bitte.
   a ■ Ich fahre mit dem Bus.
   b ■ Zahlen Sie in D-Mark?

2. Sind Sie zum ersten Mal hier?
   a ■ Nein, zum zweiten Mal.
   b ■ Ich glaube manchmal.

3. Möchten Sie nicht reden?
   a ■ Ich spreche kein Deutsch.
   b ■ Ich spreche Deutsch.

4. Gibt es hier Taxis?
   a ■ Ja, ich nehme ein Taxi.
   b ■ Ja, am Bahnhof.

3. Where is it?

*Hier ist **das Telefon**.*

1. das Telefon, hier
2. das Hotel, rechts
3. der Ausgang, dort drüben
4. der Bahnhof, links

5. die Bank, rechts
6. das Reisebüro, hier
7. das Gepäck, dort
8. der Computer, links

4. (K)ein, (k)eine or (k)einen?

1. Ich nehme ein____ Taxi.
2. Ich möchte ein____ Postkarte.
3. Haben Sie ein____ Problem?
4. Tut mir Leid, ich bin kein____ Ingenieurin.
5. Haben Sie ein____ Minute?
6. Ich nehme kein____ Flugzeug, ich nehme ein____ Zug.
7. Wir möchten ein____ Buch kaufen.
8. Ich habe kein____ Telefonkarte.
9. Bitte! Ich möchte kein____ Problem.
10. Nehmen Sie noch ein____ Rotwein?

gebucht	reserved
vor drei Tagen	three days ago
angerufen	called
finden	to find
der Pass	passport
das Frühstück	breakfast
von … bis	from … to
was kostet	how much is
der Schlüssel	key
der Stock	floor

frühstücken - the verb comes from *das Frühstück*.

Time

	die Sekunde	second
60 sec	*die Minute*	minute
60 min	*die Stunde*	hour
24 h	*der Tag*	day
7 Tage	*die Woche*	week
4 Wochen + 2–3 Tage		
	der Monat	month
12 Monate	*das Jahr*	year

Ja bitte?	Yes, please?
Guten Tag. Mein Name ist Muller.	Hello. My name is Muller.
Möchten Sie ein Zimmer?	Would you like a room?
Ja, ich habe gebucht.	Yes, I've reserved one.
Einen Moment.	Just a moment.
Ich habe vor drei Tagen angerufen.	I called three days ago.
Tut mir Leid – ich kann Sie nicht finden.	Sorry – I can't find you.
Wie?	Pardon?
Hier! Alles in Ordnung.	Here we are! It's okay.
Gut!	Good!
Kann ich Ihren Pass haben?	Can I have your passport?
Hier bitte.	Here you are.
Frühstück ist von 7 Uhr 30 bis 10 Uhr.	Breakfast is from 7.30 to 10.
Ich frühstücke nicht im Hotel.	I won't be breakfasting at the hotel.
Kein Problem.	No problem.
Ach so – was kostet das Zimmer?	Oh – How much is the room?
140 Mark. Hier sind die Schlüssel.	140 marks. Here are your keys.
Oh nein! Das Zimmer ist im 13-ten Stock!!!	Oh no! The room is on the 13th floor!!

Past :
Ich habe angeruf-en

There are also past participles which end in *-en*:

fahren	ge-fahr-en
geben	ge-geb-en
heißen	ge-heiß-en
kommen	ge-komm-en
raten	ge-rat-en
rufen	ge-ruf-en

When a verb expresses movement, the past is declined not with *haben*, but with *sein*:
Ich bin gekommen.
Sind Sie nach Berlin gefahren?

Note the following past participles:

anrufen	an-ge-rufen
wegfahren	weg-ge-fahren
einkaufen	ein-ge-kauft
einchecken	ein-ge-checkt
zurückrufen	zurück-ge-rufen

1. Sort into matching pairs

1. das Frühstück
2. unbedingt
3. reden
4. schulden
5. der Schlüssel

a ■ the key
b ■ to owe
c ■ really
d ■ the breakfast
e ■ to talk

2. Fill in the gaps

1. Ich bin nicht mit dem Flugzeug _ _ _ _ _ _ _ _.
2. Ich habe Ihnen das Geschenk _ _ _ _ _ _ _.
3. Sie wissen das nicht? Haben Sie alles _ _ _ _ _ _ _ _?
4. Wir sind vor drei Tagen nach Frankfurt _ _ _ _ _ _ _.
5. Haben Sie im Hotel _ _ _ _ _ _ _ _ _?
6. Ich habe ein Zimmer _ _ _ _ _ _ _ _.
7. Sind Sie müde, haben Sie viel _ _ _ _ _ _ _ _ _?
8. Sie brauchen kein Geld. Ich habe die Pizza für Sie _ _ _ _ _ _.
9. Wir haben in der Buchhandlung ein schönes Buch _ _ _ _ _ _.

(gekauft - bezahlt - gearbeitet - gebucht - angerufen - gefahren - vergessen - gegeben - gekommen)

3. Ask if there are any … here

Gibt es hier Taxis?
1. das Taxi 2. das Buch 3. die Briefmarke 4. das Geschenk
5. die Telefonkarte 6. der Computer 7. das Hotel 8. die Bank

4. What did you do when?

Ich bin vor drei Tagen nach München gefahren.
1. nach München fahren, vor drei Tagen
2. im Hotel anrufen, vor fünf Minuten
3. ein Fax senden, um elf
4. ein schönes Buch kaufen, vor vier Tagen
5. ins Hotel kommen, um vier Uhr
6. in Wien leben, vor zehn Jahren

5. Say how much it is

Die Fahrkarte kostet vierundfünfzig Mark.
1. Fahrkarte 54,– DM   2. Geschenk 19,– DM   3. Käse 4,50 DM
4. Telefonkarte 12,– DM   5. Weißbrot 3,80 DM   6. Zeitung 1,50 DM
7. Zimmer 90,– DM   8. Wurst 6,20 DM   9. Postkarte 1,20 DM

Hotels are the same all over the world – varying from the comfortable to the run-down. They say very little about the people of the country where they are, unlike their homes. How individuals live, i.e. how they decorate their own flats and houses tells us a great deal about them. Town centres are usually business districts where few people live and which are deserted after the shops close. Most people live in residential areas, where there is at the most a supermarket and with a bit of luck also a good baker's and a good butcher's. 60 percent of Germans live in rented property, i.e. are not home-owners. The rents are high, between 10 and 17 dollars per square metre. For those on a low income or unemployed, paying the monthly rent can become a real problem.

The better-off have their own flat or detached house on the edge of a town or a bit outside it. Germans are not especially outgoing, but sometimes the residents of a particular street get together and have parties in the summer or help each other out with babysitting. If you walk along a street of terraced houses on a warm summer evening, the tantalizing smells of a barbecue will be wafted towards you: the husband is in charge of the grill and the wife is taking care of everything else – salads, drinks, setting the table, clearing away, washing up etc.

Not everyone lives in a family, many live alone. Others, especially if they are not married and in a town, live in shared flats because it's cheaper and more fun.

Temporary accommodation

If you want to stay somewhere for a slightly longer period, i.e. one or more months, you can find a room or a furnished flat from an accommodation agency called the *Mitwohnzentrale*. The advantage of this is that you are your own boss and save money. By comparison, staying in a hotel is usually quite expensive.

20 years abroad

Gone are the days when people travelled for months on foot overland or for weeks on a sailing ship and approached their destination slowly. The journeys of the great travellers are hard to envisage now. Marco Polo allegedly took 20 years to get to China and back. And the great poet Johann Wolfgang von Goethe spent the whole of 1787 travelling in Italy, studying its natural features as well as its culture. Later he recorded his experiences in his *Italienische Reise* (Italian journey).
In the nineteenth century Alexander von Humboldt was perhaps Germany's most important traveller. He spent five years from 1799–1804 in North and South America, where he conducted biological, geographical, geological, oceanographic, ethnological and linguistic research. This man with his comprehensive knowledge of so many fields still ranks as a genius today.

Sabine Wiedenroth is a teacher and Sabine Wiedenroth is tired. Her nerves are on edge from the constant disruptions in the classroom because the children can't concentrate, from the noise in the playground and the tedious staff meetings she has to attend. Sabine Wiedenroth needs a change of scenery, so the first place to go is to a travel agency.

Ich möchte eine Reise machen, she says, (= I want to go away), and I want a quiet hotel, preferably with full board. The man in the travel agency suggests something in the South Pacific, but that's too far away for Sabine and probably too expensive. Then he suggests something in the Canary Islands, which Sabine thinks is quite a good idea. *Ja, Teneriffa, das wäre nicht schlecht* (= Yes, Tenerife, that wouldn't be a bad idea). Finally he comes up with Austria: *Vielleicht eine Reise in die Berge? Tirol – das ist sehr schön!* (= What about a trip to the mountains? Tyrol is beautiful!) Sabine likes the sound of this, makes a down payment of 100 marks and already feels better.

Nothing is worse than the feeling of being closed in. A trip shows that you are free and able to get away. A holiday used to be something unusual for most Germans, and only a few of the better-off could afford it. Today travel agencies are as popular as bargain counters in department stores when the prices have just been reduced. The world has become available to many people and one destination is much the same as any other.

tun	. . . .	to do
die Reise	. . . .	journey, trip
England	. . . .	England
in	. . . .	to, in
die Berge	. . . .	mountains
Österreich	. . . .	Austria
die Person	. . . .	person
pro Person	. . . .	per person
teuer	. . . .	expensive

Prepositions

im Zimmer	in the room
in die Berge	(in)to the mountains
mit Hotel	with a hotel
für Sie	for you
nach England	to England
am Bahnhof	at the station
aus München	from Munich

tun

ich tue	I do
er/sie tut	he/she does
wir tun	we do
Sie tun	you do

Guten Tag.	Hello.
Was kann ich für Sie tun?	What can I do for you?
Ich möchte eine Reise machen.	I want to go away.
Wohin möchten Sie fahren?	Where would you like to go?
Ich weiß nicht...	I don't know...
Vielleicht nach England?	Maybe England?
Nein, lieber in die Berge.	No, I'd rather go to the mountains.
Nach Österreich?	To Austria?
Ja, Tirol wäre gut.	Yes, Tirol would be good.
Hier – zwei Wochen mit Hotel.	Here you are – two weeks with a hotel.
Was kostet das?	How much is that?
Für wie viele Personen?	For how many persons?
Zwei Personen.	Two persons.
Das kostet DM 1190,–.	That's 1190 marks.
Zusammen?	Altogether?
Nein, pro Person.	No, per person.
Das ist nicht sehr teuer.	That's not very expensive.
Nein, das ist wirklich nicht teuer.	No, it really isn't.
Gut – buchen Sie bitte.	Good, would you please book that?
Ihre Namen?	Your name, please?

in die Berge

Don't be surprised if one time it's *im Hotel* and another time *ins Hotel*.
im (in + dem) means "in the" and
ins (in das) means "to the"
...
This is a German peculiarity: the accusative is often used to express motion *(in das)* while the dative *(in dem)* is used for position. Just so you recognize it next time.

Pro

This little word has a distributive function
1 Glas Bier pro Person
    1 glass of beer per person
20,– DM pro Tag
    20 marks a day
4 Bücher pro Klasse
    4 books per class

1. What's the plural?

You can't know all the plural forms. But you'll find them in the dictionary in the appendix.

1. die Person   die Person_ _
2. das Zimmer   die Zimmer_
3. das Taxi   die Taxi_ _
4. das Brot   die Brot_ _
5. der Pass   die P_ _ _ _

6. das Buch   die B _ _ _ _ _
7. der Zug   die Z _ _ _ _
8. das Hotel   die Hotel_ _
9. der Schlüssel   die Schlüssel_

2. The right answer   2/6

A question can also be answered with another – in this exercise and in life.

1. Frühstücken Sie im Hotel?
   a ■ Ein Zimmer mit Frühstück bitte.
   b ■ Geht es um zehn Uhr?

2. Haben Sie die Schlüssel?
   a ■ Ich kann die Schlüssel finden.
   b ■ Hier sind die Schlüssel.

3. Ich brauche unbedingt ein Taxi.
   a ■ Am besten Sie rufen an.
   b ■ Gibt es hier Züge?

4. Haben Sie gebucht?
   a ■ Haben Sie mein Fax nicht bekommen?
   b ■ Ja, ich suche ein Buch.

5. Was schulde ich Ihnen?
   a ■ Das ist schon bezahlt.
   b ■ Ich brauche eine Entschuldigung.

3. Say what you can't find   2/7

Remember *finden* takes the accusative, so *der* must become *den*.

*Ich kann **den Schlüssel** nicht finden.*

1. der Schlüssel
2. das Buch
3. die Zeitung
4. der Computer
5. der Rotwein

6. die Fahrkarte
7. der Käse
8. das Ticket
9. der Brief
10. der Zug

4. Put them together

A command can be recognized by the exclamation mark, a question by the question mark. Obvious, isn't it?

1. Was kann ich tun
2. Buchen Sie 2 Wochen
3. Bitte eine Briefmarke
4. Herr Müller ist nicht hier
5. Zahlen Sie

a ■ im Moment.
b ■ für eine Postkarte.
c ■ mit Kreditkarte?
d ■ für Sie?
e ■ mit Hotel!

warum?	....	why?
zum Beispiel	....	for example
das Flugzeug	....	plane
die Verspätung	....	delay
na ja	....	well
schlecht	....	bad
laut	....	noisy
das Wetter	....	weather
die Katastrophe	....	catastrophe
besser als	....	better than

The question *warum?* is always answered with *weil* (= because), but that will be dealt with later as it is a subordinate clause, and in that sort of clause the verb always has to go to the end. Just something to keep at the back of your mind.

The word *Verspätung* incorporates *spät* – late. The suffix *-ung* is always used to form a noun. Do you know any other words like it? *Zeitung* (= newspaper), *Achtung* (look out) etc.

na ja, this is one of those phrases that you won't find in any dictionary, although everyone says it.

Urlaub ist schön.	....	Holidays are nice.
Kommt drauf an.	....	That depends.
Warum?	....	Why do you say that?
Manchmal ist es nicht schön.	....	Sometimes they're not nice.
Ja?	....	Oh really?
Zum Beispiel: das Flugzeug hat Verspätung.	....	For example, the plane's delayed.
Na ja, was sind zwei Stunden im Leben?	....	Well, what are two hours in a lifetime?
Oder das Hotel ist schlecht und laut.		Or the hotel is bad and noisy.
Dann müssen Sie ein anderes suchen.	....	Then you have to look for another one.
Oder das Wetter ist eine Katastrophe.	....	Or the weather is catastrophic.
Ich finde, Urlaub ist besser als arbeiten.	....	I think holidays are better than working.
Ich finde das auch.	....	I think so too.

schlecht and *schlimm* – both mean bad. *Schlecht* is the opposite of *gut,* *schlimm* also has negative moral connotations.

besser (= better) is incidentally the comparative form of *gut.*
German *-ss-* often corresponds to English *-t-:*

besser	better
Wasser	water
essen	eat
lassen	let
vergessen	forget

1. Put in the right order

There are no questions in this jumble of words. We've made it a bit harder for you and left out the full stops and the capital letters at the beginning of the sentence.

1. Verspätung - das Flugzeug - drei Stunden - hat
2. gebucht - habe - eine Reise - ich
3. fahren - in die Berge - möchten - wir - nach Österreich
4. das - keine - ist - heute - Wetter - Katastrophe
5. ist - mein Zimmer - laut - schlecht - und

2. Give your opinion

Ich finde, **Urlaub ist schön.**

1. Urlaub, schön
2. das Hotel, laut
3. das Buch, interessant
4. die Zeitung, schlecht
5. der Computer, gut
6. die Idee, wunderbar
7. der Hotelmanager, neugierig
8. die Reise, schön
9. Urlaub, besser als arbeiten

Urlaub has no article here because we are talking about holidays in general. If we are talking about a specific holiday then it's *Mein Urlaub, Wie finden Sie den Urlaub?* etc.

3. Read aloud

Remember how simple ordinal numbers are? Irregular: *erster, zweiter, dritter, siebter.*
Regular: all other numbers: *vier-ter, neun-ter, siebenunddreißig-s-ter.*
Okay, the last one is not quite regular, there's an "s" before the final syllable. It's the same for all numbers ending in *-ig (zwanzig, vierzig, fünfzig …).*

1. Das ist der 12. Stock, hier ist mein Zimmer.
2. Das ist der 4. Brief von Jürgen.
3. Nehmen Sie die 3. Straße links.
4. Der 2. Rotwein ist sehr gut.
5. Das ist die 1. gute Idee.

4. Sense or nonsense? Translate

A few sentences to give you food for thought. They're a bit more interesting than *Herr Muller ist im Hotel,* aren't they?

1. I owe you an idea.
2. Is there a bank here with life?
3. Would you like a sausage at the station?
4. My computer's on holiday.
5. An apology costs nothing.

5. Give your opinion again

Finden takes the accusative. Whenever the article is *der,* it must be changed to *den.* Not really a problem, is it?

Ich finde **die Reise wunderbar.**

1. die Reise, wunderbar
2. der Hotelmanager, neugierig
3. die Idee, schön
4. der Computer, laut
5. die Zeitung, interessant
6. das Buch, schlecht
7. das Hotel, gut
8. Urlaub, schön

"The most precious weeks of the year" is the way Neckermann describes holidays. Neckermann should know, it's one of the biggest tour operators in the country. On average Germans have over six weeks' holiday a year, and most of them – at least at present – also have enough money to go away. Together with the Swiss, they are world champions in travelling: you meet Germans everywhere, by the Amazon, in Tierra del Fuego, in Black Africa or in Turkey: an annual holiday is simply part of life.

Germans prefer to go abroad, and only just over 30 % spend their holidays in their own country. When they do stay within Germany, they usually go somewhere in the south: to Bavaria, the Allgäu or the Black Forest. Tourism within Germany is otherwise going through a crisis, with the majority of people preferring to go to Austria and the Mediterranean countries: Spain, France, Italy and Greece. Overseas destinations are also becoming increasingly popular. It is almost normal to go to the USA or Thailand.

Germans are considered good tourists. Perhaps also because they don't try and beat prices right down and usually pay for everything immediately.

Holidays are also well-known as a time of crisis. All the family problems which are usually swept under the carpet tend to resurface during the dearest weeks of the year. Quite a few divorces are initiated in Indonesia, Venezuela or by Lake Wolfgang in Austria.

Bargain holidays

There are plenty of travellers who don't know until just before they leave where they're going. This is because a few days before departure it's possible to get last-minute offers for half the price. Where? In some travel agencies and at the airport. It's certainly a bit odd if you don't care whether you're going to Thailand or Cuba, but all many people want is sun and a bit of luxury, to stoke up the batteries in order to survive another year in the office.

T Test 3

1. Which is right?

Cyclists in pedestrian precincts should in fact get off and push, but none of them do.

Some car drivers don't mind traffic jams at all and don't look at all frustrated.

Here's a hint: flying is not exactly cheap.

If you don't know the answer, try it out.

What is meant is those roads which smell of barbecues on summer evenings.

We think travel broadens your own personal horizons.

1. After the shops have closed, pedestrian precincts are
   a ■ rather lifeless.
   b ■ the centre of social activity.
   c ■ taboo for roller-bladers.
2. In the summer holidays there are traffic jams on the motorways of over
   a ■ 10 km.
   b ■ 100 km.
   c ■ 1000 km.
3. The passengers on flights within Germany are
   a ■ only pensioners visiting their grandchildren.
   b ■ mainly businessmen with little time.
   c ■ only the children of divorced parents.
4. Taxis in Germany are
   a ■ particularly cheap.
   b ■ as expensive as anywhere else.
   c ■ more expensive than elsewhere.
5. Residential districts with detached houses are mainly
   a ■ in the centre of towns.
   b ■ in the country.
   c ■ on the edge of towns.
6. Travelling shows that you
   a ■ have no money to stay at home.
   b ■ don't feel closed in.
   c ■ don't like it at home.

2. Answers and questions

It's easy if you think what would be appropriate to the particular situation.

1. Wohin möchten Sie fahren?
2. Was schulde ich Ihnen?
3. Kann ich hier einchecken?
4. Kann ich mit Scheck bezahlen?
5. Sind Sie müde?
6. Wo ist der Bahnhof bitte?

a ■ Hier immer geradeaus.
b ■ Ja, ich habe viel gearbeitet.
c ■ Vielleicht nach Amerika.
d ■ Kein Problem.
e ■ Haben Sie ein Lufthansa-Ticket?
f ■ Vierzehn Mark.

3. Multiple choice

Here it's not either one or the other, but which one of three is correct.

1. Ich finde, _____ ist besser als arbeiten.
   a ■ Flugzeug
   b ■ Urlaub
   c ■ Verspätung
2. Ich _____ eine Reise machen.
   a ■ brauchen
   b ■ möchten
   c ■ möchte
3. Frühstück ist _____.
   a ■ von 8 bis 10 Uhr
   b ■ geradeaus
   c ■ in bar
4. Ich brauche _____ ein Taxi.
   a ■ anrufen
   b ■ unbedingt
   c ■ möchte
5. Am besten Sie _____ zu Ausgang 3.
   a ■ bleiben
   b ■ machen
   c ■ gehen
6. Das ist eine _____ Idee.
   a ■ guter
   b ■ gute
   c ■ guten

4. Sense and nonsense

1. Delay is expensive.
2. The telephone card is a catastrophe.
3. I need the mountains.
4. Are you taking a catastrophe?
5. Give me an airline.
6. The weather is on the 13th floor.

When you translate these sentences, it's not important whether they have any meaning. You can translate quite mechanically and correctly without understanding them. Here, however, you might think about the nonsense and perhaps you'll find a situation where a particular sentence would in fact have some meaning.

Normal breakfast

Brot	bread
Brötchen	roll
Butter	butter
Margarine	margarine
Marmelade	jam
Kaffee	coffee
Tee	tea
Milch	milk
Kakao	cocoa

Special breakfast

Käse	cheese
Wurst	sausage
Schinken	ham
Ei	egg
Orangensaft	orange juice

Natural breakfast

Honig	honey
Joghurt	yoghurt
Quark	curd cheese
Müsli	muesli

Luxury breakfast

Lachs	salmon
Kaviar	caviar
Sekt	champagne

The health-conscious grind their grains in the evening, soak them overnight and breakfast on a kind of healthy porridge.

In Bavaria, for example, hot white sausage (Weißwurst) is served in the morning. But woe betide anyone who orders it after midday. In Bavaria there is no worse sin.

Breakfast is a great cultural divide. North Europeans love it and "make a meal" of it. The French, Spanish and Italians limit it to the essentials. Breakfast in Germany is a ritual, without which the world would come to an end. There are people who get up at say half past seven, regular as clockwork, but who suddenly find themselves one day having to struggle out of bed at quarter past four in the morning to go away on a trip. What do they do? Sit down at this unearthly hour to have a good solid breakfast first. In the middle of the night.

What the Germans like best is fresh bread rolls. What they put on them is a matter of taste. Some have a sweet tooth and prefer jam or honey. Others like something with a bit more body to it: sausage, ham, fish or cheese. Almost everyone starts the weekend with breakfast. This might be a social occasion: people meet for a late breakfast in a hotel (brunch is a new German word), café or at someone's home. And chat about their private lives and their work. The important thing is being together with other people. Business people have managed to combine their economic interests with their pleasure in breakfast: Arbeitsfrühstück (= working breakfast) is what it's called, and export figures and new investments are discussed over coffee and rolls.

Kaffee ist fertig (= Coffee's ready) – this is the signal to all those who have slept under the same roof to gather round the table. And the question put to the guest, Was möchten Sie frühstücken? (= What would you like for breakfast?) expresses the innate respect of the Germans for other tastes in breakfast.

der Kaffee	coffee
fertig	ready
gehört	heard
schon	already
geschlafen	slept
das Müsli	muesli
gesund	healthy
die Milch	milk
der Zucker	sugar
schmecken	to taste, taste good

fertig has several meanings: 1. ready 2. finished 3. shattered.

schon (basic meaning = already) is another of those words that is often just put in for emphasis, and can't necessarily be translated. Here it expresses a slight irritation ...

Müsli is a Swiss invention, consisting of rolled oats, raisins and nuts etc. eaten with fruit, yoghurt or milk. Doctors say it's very healthy because it contains so much roughage.

Kaffee ist fertig!	Coffee's ready!
Ich komme.	I'm coming.
Kaffee ist fertig !!!	Coffee's ready!!!
Ich hab's gehört. Ich komme ja schon.	I heard. I'm on my way.
Guten Morgen.	Good morning.
Guten Morgen.	Good morning.
Haben Sie gut geschlafen?	Did you sleep well?
Danke, sehr gut.	Yes, very well thank you.
Was möchten Sie frühstücken?	What would you like for breakfast?
Geben Sie mir bitte Müsli.	I'd like some muesli, please.
Hier. Das ist sehr gesund.	Here you are. That's very healthy.
Danke schön.	Thank you very much.
Den Kaffee mit Milch?	Do you take milk in your coffee?
Ja, und viel Zucker.	Yes, and lots of sugar.
Das ist nicht so gesund.	That's not so healthy.
Aber es schmeckt.	But it tastes good.

Haben Sie gut geschlafen? (= Did you sleep well?) This is a question you ask a guest. It's rather a strange thing to say really, isn't it?

Den Kaffee mit Milch

Why is it *den* and not *der*? Because the sentence is short for *Möchten Sie den Kaffee mit Milch?*

1. Make a recommendation

Hier ist **Käse**. *Der ist* **sehr gut**.

1. Käse, sehr gut
2. Vollkornbrot, gesund
3. Rotwein, wunderbar
4. Wurst, nicht schlecht
5. Buch, interessant
6. Postkarte, schön
7. Idee, sehr gut
8. Zeitung, nicht schlecht

Food items have no article, when the quantity is inde-terminate. While in English we would say "some cheese", in German the noun is not qualified in any way. From the 5th sentence on you must put *ein/eine* in front of the noun because it is something specific.

2   Ask a favour

Geben *Sie mir bitte* **einen Kaffee**.

1. einen Kaffee, geben
2. eine Fahrkarte, kaufen
3. Bescheid, sagen
4. eine Pizza, machen
5. mit Kreditkarte, zahlen
6. drei Briefmarken, geben
7. das Hotel, finden
8. die Reise, buchen

Bitte can also come in the middle of the sentence after *mir*.

3. Find the partners

1. Haben Sie gut geschlafen?
2. Haben Sie schon gefrühstückt?
3. Haben Sie gehört?
4. Haben Sie die Frage verstanden?
5. Haben Sie das geglaubt?

a ■ Have you heard?
b ■ Did you believe that?
c ■ Have you already had breakfast?
d ■ Did you understand the question?
e ■ Did you sleep well?

Identify the correct transla-tion for each sentence. Does the exercise seem too easy? The idea is to help you familiarize yourself with the past tense.

4. Find the right answer

1. Frühstück ist fertig!

a ■ Ich komme schon.
b ■ Ich habe gut geschlafen.

2. Haben Sie gut geschlafen?

a ■ Danke, es geht.
b ■ Ich habe geschlafen.

3. Möchten Sie Zucker im Kaffee?

a ■ Nein, das ist nicht gesund.
b ■ Nein, ich möchte Müsli.

4. Haben Sie gehört?

a ■ Natürlich.
b ■ Sonst noch was?

All the questions can be used at breakfast. The re-sponse to no. 4 can be used by anyone reading the paper and not really listening.

darf ich	may I
die Tasse	cup
gerne	gladly
ich hätte gern	I would like
das Ei	egg
gekocht	boiled
Bescheid sagen	to tell somebody
die Küche	kitchen
unser	our
der Bäcker	baker

Darf ich Ihnen noch
eine Tasse Kaffee geben? .... May I give you another
cup of coffee?
Ja, gerne. .... Yes, please.
Sonst noch was? .... Anything else?
Ja, ich hätte gern ein Ei. .... Yes, I would like an egg.
Gekocht? .... Boiled?
Natürlich, vier Minuten,
wenn's geht. .... Of course, four minutes
if that's all right.
Ich sage Bescheid in der Küche. I'll tell them in the kitchen.
Mmh, das Brot schmeckt
sehr gut. .... Mmm, the bread tastes
very good.
Ja, unser Bäcker ist wunderbar. .. Yes, our baker's wonderful.

Ja gerne –

Möchten Sie noch einen
Kognak? – Ja, gerne.
(= Would you like another
cognac? – Yes please.)
Darf ich Ihnen meine
Telefonnummer geben? –
Ja, gerne. (= Yes, please do.)
Kommen Sie mit ins Hotel?
Ja, gerne. (= Yes, I'd like to.)

Gerne is another of those
words that cannot be translated directly. *Ja gerne* is a
way of emphasizing your
positive reaction to something. The opposite is *Nein,*
danke.

Ich hätte gerne –
I would like …

is appropriate in a shop, at
the table and when you've
won the lottery: *Ich hätte*
gerne einen roten Ferrari!

If you know the breakfast
words on page 86 then
nothing can go wrong – at
least at breakfast. Unless
the toast burns, the milk
boils over and the butter is
rancid.

Sonst noch was?

Remember this expression?
It's also used in shops, see
page 47.

The little words that are missing all have something to do with breakfast.

1. What's missing?

1. Guten Morgen. Haben Sie gut _____?
2. Was _____ Sie frühstücken?
3. Ich _____ gerne einen Kaffee.
4. Das Brot ist vom _____ .
5. Noch eine _____ Kaffee?

If you are ever unemployed and have to work as a waiter in a German café, these expressions will be useful.

2. Gastronomic translation

1. Kaffee mit Milch
2. Obst mit Zucker
3. Pizza mit Käse
4. Brot mit Schinken
5. Müsli mit Joghurt
6. Tee mit Zucker
7. Frühstück mit Saft
8. Quark mit Marmelade

Look at sentence 8: *ich hätte gerne* is always followed by the accusative. You could also say that the answer to the question *was?* (= what?) is in the accusative.
Incidentally, this expression always sounds elegant and is the right thing to say in a shop or a restaurant.

3. What would you like?

*Ich hätte gerne **eine schöne Küche**.*
1. eine schöne Küche
2. ein Ticket nach Wien
3. die Kreditkarte von Bill Clinton
4. keine Katastrophe mit meiner Frau
5. Reiseschecks in Rubel
6. eine schöne Pizza
7. ein Vier-Minuten-Ei
8. einen roten Ferrari

Form questions in the past tense. Any problems? You can refresh your memory by turning to pages 63 and 70.

4. Put in the past tense

*Haben Sie **das geglaubt?***
1. das glauben
2. die Frage vergessen
3. gut schlafen
4. in Bern leben
5. das hören
6. Bescheid sagen

All the sentences, and in fact all German sentences (with the exception of questions and subordinate clauses) have one thing in common: the verb comes second.

5. Scrambled eggs

1. ja - ich - schon - komme _____
2. ist - gesund - sehr - Vollkornbrot _____
3. schmeckt - Frühstück - gut - Müsli - mit _____
4. Küche - ich - sage - der - Bescheid - in _____
5. gerne - ich - Vier-Minuten-Ei - hätte - ein _____

According to an old wives' tale we should breakfast like a king, lunch like a merchant and dine like a beggar. Not everyone can follow this advice, some people just can't face anything solid first thing. And in any case, ideas about eating habits are constantly changing, each time another scientist serves up a discovery that turns all previous findings on their head.

Thinking about nutrition is a luxury of the rich world – in our industrialized countries food is not something there is a shortage of. If anyone isn't getting enough food, this usually has psychological causes. Ideals of female beauty are such that almost any woman can find a reason for complexes: a small bosom, a big bosom, fat legs, thin legs, big eyes, small eyes ... At least as far as her figure is concerned, she can do something about remedying things by eating differently. Spring is the signal for spring-cleaning and a diet to get rid of the winter fat. All the papers are full of suggestions: only raw food, only cooked vegetables, only lean meat or only rice. No journalist, however, suggests that the most reliable way of dieting is simply to eat half what you usually do.

Nor are men now any different from women in this respect. They are also in pursuit of their ideal, go conscientiously to the fitness studio twice a week, cycle for hours in the woods and drink at the most a mineral water in the evenings "in order to keep their looks". If this boosts their confidence and improves their chances on the marriage market, good luck to them ...

Did you know ...

... that 20% of the world's population is chronically undernourished.

... that in rich countries there are people who go to health farms and pay a lot of money in order to be given nothing to eat.

Germans drink more coffee than any other nation in the world. Of course German coffee is weaker than Italian espresso, but not as weak as the American variety. According to statistics, every year Germans drink an average of around 180 litres (317 pints) of coffee per person. That's half a litre or a little under a pint a day.

The café in German-speaking countries is a meeting place. In general people do not go there to drink alcohol, and in the evenings it closes its doors before the beer cellars and wine bars. Best known are the cafés in Vienna, which are associated with the literati and splendid cakes such as *Sachertorte,* a rich chocolate cake.

It was not, as commonly believed, after the siege of Vienna by the Turks that coffee was first introduced into Europe: it was already known here fifty years before. The first European coffeehouse was opened in Venice in 1647, although it was another thirty years before a similar establishment began offering the black brew in Hamburg. The coffeehouse soon became an important meeting place for artists, musicians and journalists, among others. Generations of revolutionaries have sat in cafés, analysing everything, as well as missing the revolution in the process.

The whole point of a café is that people meet and exchange views. Visits to cafés are not usually brief items on a hectic daily agenda, but leisurely affairs: some people turn the café into their second living room and spend hours there daily with newspapers and cigarettes, playing games of chess or writing their diary and sorting out the problems of the world with other customers.

Older, mostly well-upholstered ladies enjoy café visits because of the selection of cakes and pastries – for which the German-speaking countries have an excellent reputation. Specialities such as cheesecake and Black Forest cherry cake are known all over the world. *Kommen Sie mit?* (= Are you coming?) is thus an invitation always worth accepting.

mitkommen .... to come (with)
etwas .... something
trinken .... to drink
das Café .... café
nämlich .... actually, in fact
der Hunger .... hunger
zu Fuß .... on foot
das Auto .... car
einladen .... to invite
nötig .... necessary

Kommen Sie mit? .... Are you coming with me?
Wohin? .... Where to?
Etwas trinken. .... To drink something.
Ja, gerne. .... Yes, I'd like to.
Ich weiß ein schönes Café. ..... I know a nice café.
Gut, ich habe nämlich Hunger. .. Good, I'm hungry actually.
Gehen wir zu Fuß? .... Shall we walk?
Nein, ich habe mein Auto hier. .. No, I've got my car here.
Ja? .... Have you?
Ja, wir können mit
dem Auto fahren. .... Yes, we can go by car.
Aber ich möchte Sie einladen. ... This is my treat though.
Nein, das ist nicht nötig. .... No, that's not necessary.

Separable verbs

This phenomenon first came up in Unit 5 (anrufen, zurückrufen): some verbs have a little prefix which is detached and put at the end of the sentence. For example mitkommen: **Kommen** Sie morgen um neun Uhr **mit?** Here there are only five words between kommen and mit, but there could be more: Ich **rufe** Herrn Dietmar Müller heute morgen um elf Uhr im Hotel Metropolis **zurück.**

The drink is der Kaffee (stress on the first syllable), the place is das Café (stress on the last syllable).

A word like nämlich doesn't really belong here. It is very idiomatic and can't be translated literally. It means "actually", "in fact", "for", "to put it precisely", etc.

Exception: **zu** Fuß. Normally it's **mit** dem Auto, **mit** dem Flugzeug, **mit** dem Taxi etc.

Aber ich möchte Sie einladen – literally: But I would like to invite you.

Das ist nicht nötig is an expression which shows that people find it hard to enjoy things. Instead of saying schön, sehr nett!, they diminish the value of the invitation.

1. Say it simply

*Ich **komme** morgen **mit**.*

1. Ich möchte morgen mitkommen.
2. Ich möchte Sie heute Abend anrufen.
3. Ich möchte bei Lufthansa einchecken.
4. Ich möchte Frau Krug jetzt zurückrufen.
5. Ich möchte für drei Monate wegfahren.

This is to help you practise the use of separable verbs. When they occur with *möchte* they go to the end of the sentence and are not separated. When they occur on their own, the verb root comes in second place while the separated prefix goes to the end of the sentence.

2. Find the right translation

1. Fahren wir mit dem ICE.
2. Nehmen wir das Flugzeug.
3. Gehen wir zu Fuß.
4. Fahren wir mit dem Auto.

a ■ Let's walk.
b ■ Let's go by plane.
c ■ Let's take the Intercity Express.
d ■ Let's go by car.

All the means of getting about that you've learnt, repeated as part of a suggestion.

3. Which answer is right?

1. Ich weiß ein schönes Café.
   a ■ Danke nein, ich möchte jetzt nichts trinken.
   b ■ Dort ist ein Café.

2. Haben Sie Hunger?
   a ■ Ich habe nämlich Hunger.
   b ■ Nein, ich möchte aber etwas trinken.

3. Fahren wir mit dem Auto?
   a ■ Ja, das ist ein Auto.
   b ■ Lieber mit dem Taxi.

4. Darf ich Sie einladen?
   a ■ Nein, bitte nicht.
   b ■ Ja, ich lade ein.

Don't fall into the trap, but think very carefully.

4. Say no

*__Nein__, ich möchte Ihnen **nichts** sagen.*

1. Möchten Sie mir etwas sagen?
2. Möchten Sie mir etwas geben?
3. Möchten Sie mir etwas raten?
4. Möchten Sie mir etwas wünschen?
5. Möchten Sie mir etwas zahlen?

Some people have a speech defect – they can't say no. This exercise is a combination of grammar and self-assertion training.

was darf es sein?	....	may I take your order?
zuerst	....	first
das Getränk	....	drink
für mich	....	for me
die Cola	....	coke
zu essen	....	to eat
die Bratwurst	....	(fried) sausage
der Kuchen	....	cake
uns	....	us
das Käsebrot	....	(open) cheese sandwich
nett	....	nice

Guten Tag.	....	Good afternoon.
Tag, was darf es sein?	....	Hello, can I take your order?
Wir haben ein bisschen Hunger.		We're a bit hungry.
Zuerst die Getränke bitte.	......	First the drinks, please.
Also, für mich einen Tee...	.....	A tea for me...
Einen Tee.	....	A tea.
... und für meinen Freund eine Cola.	....	... and a coke for my friend.
Und zu essen?	....	And to eat?
Haben Sie Hamburger?	....	Do you have hamburgers?
Tut mir Leid, haben wir nicht.	..	Sorry, we haven't.
Haben Sie Pizza?	....	Do you have pizza?
Auch nicht.	....	No, we don't have them either.
Haben Sie Bratwürste?	....	Do you have sausages?
Auch nicht.	....	No, we don't have them either.
Was haben Sie?	....	What do you have?
Wir haben nur Kuchen.	....	We just have cakes.
Können Sie uns nicht ein Käsebrot machen?	....	Can't you make us a cheese sandwich?
Ich frage mal in der Küche.	.....	I'll ask in the kitchen.
Danke, sehr nett.	....	Thank you, that's very nice of you.

Was darf es sein? – literally "what may it be?"

Guten Tag – remember it can be used all day until the evening.
Tag – the rather more informal greeting.

für + accusative

für mich	for me
für Sie	for you
für uns	for us

irregular: essen

ich esse	I eat
Sie essen	you eat
er/sie isst	he/she eats
wir essen	we eat

The third person (*er, sie, es*) is often irregular, i.e. the verb root is different. This also applies to the second person (*du*), which you will not meet until the end of this book.

It is the custom, not only in Germany, to order the drinks first. The meal takes longer to prepare – unless they just put it in the microwave.

If you go to a *Café* and want to eat *Wurst* or *Hamburger* you're in the wrong place. But open sandwiches and other substantial snacks are available. In the afternoon *Kaffee und Kuchen* is a widespread institution, an occasion to get together with friends.

Some waiters are afraid of the kitchen staff, and hence very careful what they offer the customer.

A pronoun in the accusative must not always have a preposition in front of it (1–7), it can also come right after the verb (8).

1. Supply the accusative

1. Haben Sie etwas für _____? (ich)
2. Kein Problem, ich suche ein Hotel für _____. (Sie)
3. Kaufen Sie bitte zwei Bücher für _____. (wir)
4. Für _____ bitte einen Kaffee. (ich)
5. Meine Frau kocht immer für _____. (wir)
6. Ich habe ein Geschenk für _____ gekauft. (Sie)
7. Ich zahle für _____. (ich)
8. Vergessen Sie _____, ich bin verheiratet. (ich)

It's always easier to translate into your own language than the other way round. Imagine if you were doing a test where you had to translate these sentences into German. Then you might be doing some looking up ....

2. Translate into English

1. Ich möchte etwas zu essen. _____
2. Gehen wir lieber zu Fuß. _____
3. Bitte zuerst die Getränke! _____
4. Wir kochen in der Küche. _____
5. Ich möchte nämlich essen. _____
6. Wir können mein Auto nehmen. _____

Sentences 1–4 are in the plural, 5–8 in the singular, so take care with kein / keine / keinen

3. You are the waiter in an empty restaurant

*Tut mir Leid, wir haben **keine Getränke**.*

1. Getränke   2. Hamburger   3. Pizzas
4. Bratwürste   5. Zucker   6. Kaffee
7. Milch   8. Tee

A helping hand:

einladen	eingeladen
hören	gehört
kochen	gekocht
sagen	gesagt
schlafen	geschlafen
zahlen	gezahlt

Don't forget that the past participle always comes right at the end.

Beware the trap!

4. Say what someone has done …

*Sie haben **gut geschlafen**.*

1. Sie schlafen gut.   2. Sie kochen etwas zu essen.
3. Sie sagen in der Küche Bescheid. 4. Sie hören die Frage nicht.
5. Sie laden mich ein.   6. Sie zahlen das Frühstück.

5. Answers and questions

1. Gehen wir etwas trinken?   a ▪ Ja, es ist noch Kuchen da.
2. Darf ich Sie einladen?   b ▪ Lieber mit dem Auto.
3. Haben Sie Pizza?   c ▪ Nein, wir haben nur Kuchen.
4. Haben Sie Kuchen?   d ▪ Nein, das ist nicht nötig.
5. Gehen wir zu Fuß?   e ▪ Sehr gute Idee!

Hospitality north of the Alps is not as important a part of the culture as it is for example amongst the Greeks and Arabs. It is only when you have got to know someone better that you might expect to be invited to their home. But there are plenty of other opportunities to meet friends: in a café in the daytime, or in a restaurant for a meal at lunchtime or in the evening. The Germans, it might be worth remembering, tend to pay separately. In other words, someone who evidently has more money does not automatically pay for all the others, unless he has specifically issued an invitation beforehand.

When business partners from different firms get together, then usually the host or the partner from the place where the meeting has been organized pays. This won't put him out of pocket, he will get it back from the firm. If he's self-employed, he can deduct it from his taxes.

In the evening people do not just meet to eat, but also to go, for example, to the cinema or the theatre – which of course requires a high level of German. A concert may be easier than the theatre; music is still the most universal language. The Germans are incidentally very popular with foreign musicians as concert audiences because they are very disciplined and concentrate. It is advisable to be punctual for cultural events. Sometimes – especially at the opera – the doors are shut after the performance starts. Latecomers then have to wait for the first interval before they are let in.

People often meet for a glass of beer or wine. In Southern Germany there are any number of *Weinstuben* (= wine bars) and *Bierkneipen* (= pubs/bars specializing in beer), often with regular customers who've made the place their "local". Beer drinkers like draught beer, and the waiter usually puts the glass down on a cardboard beer mat, making a mark on it for every glass of beer a customer drinks. In this way the waiter knows who's had what when it comes to paying. A generous person treats his friends and fellow-drinkers to a round: *Die nächste Runde geht auf mich* (= I'm paying the next round).

Many foreigners work in the catering trade. If you want to know what country your waiter comes from, see what language he adds the bill up in. People almost always add up in their mother tongue.

Don't worry, in *Weinstuben* and *Bierkneipen* you can also get non-alcoholic drinks.

There are some foods with very curious names. If you want to know what they are, you must ask a German; these are just translations:

Handkäse mit Musik
  Hand cheese with music
Halber Hahn
           Half a cockerel
Falscher Hase   False hare
Apfel im Schlafrock
  Apple in a dressing gown
Verlorene Eier   Lost eggs
Null-Diät   Zero diet
Kalter Hund   Cold dog
Berliner Weiße mit Schuss
    Berlin white with shot

German cuisine does not have a worldwide reputation, nor is it to be found everywhere like Italian, Chinese or Indian cuisine. The best-known German dish is probably sauerkraut: finely shredded, pickled white cabbage. It was very important for sailors, as it has a high vitamin C content and for a long time was the only food that prevented scurvy. Today Germans are known in the English-speaking world as Krauts.

Although German dishes are not particularly well-known, this does not mean that the country's cuisine is bland and insignificant. Leaving aside the gourmet restaurants, the cuisine generally gets better the farther south you go. An important and almost omnipresent item is the potato, which originated in South America. It is to be found in numerous variations: boiled, baked, roasted, puréed, au gratin, as soup, or even as a sweet cake. And of course, like everywhere else in the world, as chips.

One thing that is well-known about German food is the variety of *Wurst* (sausage). Sausages are usually named after the place they originally came from: Frankfurter, Wiener, Thüringer, Nürnberger, Krakauer etc. Sausages are a science in themselves.

Germany, Austria and Switzerland are linked by a common language. But each country has its own culinary characteristics and – perhaps through the influence of the French – Swiss cuisine is considered to be of particularly high quality.

If you don't know what to eat, you have to ask the waiter *Was empfehlen Sie uns?* (= What do you recommend?). The rest is luck. When the waiter says, *Kommt sofort* (= Right away), then it's advisable to be patient, as *sofort* is a relative concept …

bringen	. . . .	to bring
sofort	. . . .	right away
das Wasser	. . . .	water
empfehlen	. . . .	to recommend
der rheinische Sauerbraten	. . . .	braised beef Rhineland style
als	. . . .	as
die Vorspeise	. . . .	starter
die Champignon-Creme-Suppe		cream of mushroom soup
der Blätterteig-Broccoli	. . . .	pastry filled with broccoli
auf keinen Fall	. . . .	on no account, definitely not
die Pilz-Allergie	. . . .	mushroom allergy

Guten Abend, meine Herren.	. . .	Good evening, gentlemen.
Guten Abend.	. . . .	Good evening.
Was darf ich Ihnen bringen?	. . . .	What can I bring you?
Vielleicht zwei Sherry.	. . . .	Perhaps two sherries.
Kommt sofort.	. . . .	Right away.
Und ein Wasser bitte!!	. . . .	And a glass of water please!!
Was wünschen Sie zu essen?	. . . .	What would you like to eat?
Was empfehlen Sie uns?	. . . .	What do you recommend?
Vielleicht einen rheinischen Sauerbraten?	. . . .	Perhaps braised beef Rhineland style?
Ja, sehr gut. Zweimal bitte.	. . . . . .	Yes, very good. We'll both have that.
Und als Vorspeise?	. . . .	What would you like as a starter?
Ich weiß nicht...	. . . .	I don't know...
Champignon-Creme-Suppe mit Blätterteig-Broccoli?	. . . .	Cream of mushroom soup and puff-pastry filled with broccoli?
Nein, auf keinen Fall.	. . . .	No, definitely not.
Ja, dann vielleicht...	. . . .	Well, then maybe...
Ich habe nämlich eine Pilz-Allergie.	. . . .	You see, I've got a mushroom allergy.
Oh, Entschuldigung.	. . . .	Oh, I'm sorry.

kommt sofort –
That's what waiters always say, and it still takes half an hour. Literal translation: It's coming right away.

Dative pronouns

ich	→	*mir*
Sie	→	*Ihnen*
wir	→	*uns*

Was wünschen Sie zu essen in fact sounds very old-fashioned. This is what you might hear in four-star restaurants. Usually what the waiter says is *Was möchten Sie essen,* or when you've put the menu down: *Haben Sie schon etwas ausgewählt?* (= Have you already chosen something?)

Compound words

It's a common feature of German to just put two nouns together and make a new word with a meaning of its own e.g. die *Pilz-Allergie* (*der Pilz* = mushroom). Note that the last word is always the important one - it determines the article (*der/die/das*) and the meaning. Sometimes three or more words are strung together: *Champignon-Creme-Suppe.* This is not of course a mushroom but a soup. What kind of soup? One made of creamed mushrooms.

auf keinen Fall

This always sounds very convincing and is much stronger than a simple *nein.*

1. Give the English for the following

Here's a list of compound words. You'll have no problem understanding all the individual parts, so you'll also be able to understand the whole word. Some of the words are written together as one word, but to make it easier for you they're printed here with a hyphen and capital letters.

1. die Pilz-Allergie _____
2. das Käse-Brot _____
3. die Bank-Karte _____
4. die Butter-Milch _____
5. die Milch-Suppe _____
6. die Kaffee-Tasse _____
7. die Fahr-Karte _____

8. das Zucker-Brot _____
9. das Urlaubs-Wetter _____
10. das Maschinen-Problem ___
11. der Reise-Scheck _____
12. der Zimmer-Schlüssel _____
13. die Journalisten-Frau _____
14. die Computer-Zeitung ___

2. You are the waiter in a five-star-restaurant   2/23

Change the definite article *(der/die/das)* to the indefinite and put it in the accusative. *(einen/eine/ein)*

Darf ich Ihnen noch **einen Sherry** *bringen?*
1. der Sherry
2. der Rotwein
3. der Sauerbraten
4. die Käse-Pizza
5. die Broccoli-Creme-Suppe mit Käse-Blätterteig
6. die Bratwurst
7. die Vorspeise
8. die zweite Vorspeise
9. der Kuchen

3. Questions and answers

How do you find these exercises, do you get on better listening to them or reading them?

1. Was empfehlen Sie uns?
   a ■ Vielleicht einen Sauerbraten.
   b ■ Ich habe keinen Sauerbraten.

2. Was wünschen Sie zu essen?
   a ■ Haben Sie Champignon-Suppe?
   b ■ Ich habe nur Champignon-Suppe.

3. Und als Vorspeise?
   a ■ Ich möchte keine Vorspeise.
   b ■ Ich mache ein Reise.

4. Darf ich Ihnen einen Sherry bringen?
   a ■ Ich trinke keinen Saft.
   b ■ Ja, gerne.

4. Give the German translation

Survival kit for a German restaurant.

1. On no account. _____
2. Right away. _____
3. What would you like as a starter? _____
4. I have a cheese allergy. _____
5. Can you bring me a (fried) sausage? _____
6. I'm sorry, I haven't got that. _____

die Rechnung . . . bill	hatten . . . . had
waren . . . . were	stimmt so . . . . that's all right
die Quittung . . . . receipt	die Karte . . . . menu
sehen . . . . to see	noch mal . . . . again
das Trinkgeld . . . tip	

Kann ich zahlen bitte? . . . . Can I have the bill please?
Ich komme sofort. . . . . I'll be with you right away.
Zahlen bitte! . . . . The bill please!
Komm sofort. . . . . Right away.
Die R-e-c-h-n-u-n-g bitte!!! . . . . . The b-i-l-l please!!!
Sofort. Ja, was hatten Sie? . . . . . . Right away. Yes, what did you have?
Das waren zwei Sauerbraten
und eine Suppe. . . . . Two Sauerbraten and one soup.
Was hatten Sie zu trinken? . . . . . What did you have to drink?
Wir hatten zwei Wein und ein Wasser. We had two (glasses of) wine
and one (bottle of) water.

Das macht ... einen Moment... That's ... just a moment...
Ich glaube, wir hatten zwei Wasser. I think we had two bottles of water.
Okay, 20,50, 41,–, 46,50,
53,50 ... 57,50 bitte. . . . . Okay, 20.50, 41, 46.50,
53.50, ... 57.50 please.

Hier haben Sie sechzig. Stimmt so. . . Here's sixty. Keep the change.
Danke schön. Brauchen Sie
eine Quittung? . . . . Thank you very much.
Do you need a receipt?
Ja, das wäre nett. . . . . Yes, that would be nice.
Hier, Ihre Quittung. . . . . Here's your receipt.
Moment mal, kann ich die Karte
noch mal sehen? . . . . Just a moment, can I see the menu again?
Natürlich... . . . . Of course...
Hier – der Sauerbraten kostet
nur 18,– Mark. . . . . Here – the Sauerbraten costs
only 18 marks.

Oh Entschuldigung. Sie bekommen
noch fünf Mark zurück. . . . . Oh sorry. You get five marks back.
Nein, das ist Okay. . . . . No, that's all right.
Vielen Dank. Auf Wiedersehen. . . Thank you very much. Goodbye.
Oh, jetzt habe ich
7,50 Trinkgeld gegeben. . . . . Oh, now I've given a 7.50 tip.

A new past tense
There is another past tense:
the imperfect. It is used
mainly in written German,
and in North Germany it is
also used in the spoken
language. The imperfect
forms of *haben* and *sein*,
the two most important
occurrences of this tense,
can be heard all the time.

haben
ich hatte
er/sie hatte
Sie hatten
wir hatten

sein
ich war
er/sie war
Sie waren
wir waren

**Zwei Wein
und ein Wasser**
You don't have to say if it
came in a glass or a bottle.
And it's singular, even if it's
plural: *zwei Bier* (= two
beer)!

stimmt so
Stimmt means "that's right".
Stimmt so is used in the
sense of "The rest is for
you".

Trinkgeld
Normally you always round
up the bill. But if your bill is
for example 21 marks, then
30 marks would be too
much. So what you say is
*Geben Sie mir bitte auf
23 Mark raus* (= Please
give me change for
23 marks) or 24 or 25.
Rausgeben or *herausgeben*
is a separable verb and
means to give someone
their change.

2/25

1. Put in the past tense

Please say these sentences as if everything had already happened.

1. Ich bin in Köln. _____
2. Haben Sie schon Urlaub? _____
3. Wir sind neugierig. _____
4. Sind Sie im Hotel? _____
5. Herr Muller ist Journalist. _____
6. Ich bin verheiratet. _____

2. Which question is right?

Too much routine is a bad thing. Here we have turned the questions and answers round so you have to pick out the right question.

1. Ja, unbedingt.   a ■ Brauchen Sie
                                      eine Quittung?
                               b ■ Haben Sie die Rechnung?
2. Hier bitte.   a ■ Kann ich die Karte
                                      noch mal sehen?
                               b ■ Kann ich Ihnen
                                      die Karte bringen?
3. Ich glaube, ich hatte sieben Wein. a ■ Was hatten Sie zu trinken?
                               b ■ Was hatten Sie zu essen?
4. Danke schön, sehr nett.   a ■ Geben Sie Trinkgeld?
                               b ■ Hier, stimmt so.

3. Adding up the bill

Repetition of the numbers combined with a little brainwork just to keep that grey matter ticking over. Prices like these would be found in ordinary restaurants, but a restaurant in the city centre usually costs 50–100 % more.

Zwei Wein – sieben Mark, ein Wasser – drei Mark.
Macht zusammen zehn Mark.
1. 2 Wein à DM 3,50, 1 Wasser à DM 3,–
2. 1 Pizza à DM 11,–, ein Bier à DM 4,20
3. 3 Käsebrote à DM 6,–, 3 Wasser à DM 2,50
4. 2 Bratwürste à DM 4,50, 1 Cola à DM 3,–
5. 4 Hamburger à DM 4,–, 1 Wein à DM 4,50
6. 2 Wasser à DM 3,–, 1 Suppe à DM 7,–
7. 5 Schinkenbrote à DM 6,50, 5 Cola à DM 2,40

4. Put in the first person

Practise speaking, and at the same time go over the first person again.

Ich empfehle Sauerbraten.
1. Sie empfehlen Sauerbraten.
2. Sie essen heute nichts.
3. Sie bringen die Karte.
4. Sie zahlen zwei Wein.
5. Sie kommen sofort.
6. Sie geben kein Trinkgeld.

Bier auf Wein – das lass sein; Wein auf Bier – das rat' ich dir (= Beer after wine – don't ever touch it; wine after beer – I can advise that). As you can see, alcohol has developed its own philosophy, and there's always an excuse for a drink. Quite a few people, however, overdo it and become addicted; alcoholism is a widespread addictive illness from which some people never recover.

Every culture has its own drugs: the Romans brought wine to Germany, the Teutons developed beer and the Christian monasteries specialized in the production of spirits and liqueurs.

Anyone who likes drinking will always find an occasion to do so. When for example one of the employees in a firm has a birthday, then this is a reason for everyone to get together for a drink before lunch at eleven or half-past eleven. Usually *Sekt* is drunk, a sort of German champagne. To make the drink less obvious, it is mixed with orange juice, and then looks quite harmless, in fact non-alcoholic.

It only starts to get difficult when the boss is an alcoholic and everyone knows he's got a bottle of cognac concealed in his desk, but no-one dares say anything. The point at which alcoholism becomes a problem is in fact when the drink has noticeable effects on the person concerned and they can't work properly, become forgetful and unreliable. Then the only thing that will help is usually withdrawal treatment and the will to stay "dry" thereafter.

Social occasions, especially in the evening, are almost always accompanied in Germany by beer and wine, and in more elegant circles also by *Sekt* or champagne. This makes it difficult for a former drinker, who has to refuse and is very well aware that one exception will lead to a relapse.

Simply prohibiting alcohol would be no answer either. Hundreds of thousands of wine-growers, beer brewers and drinks firms make a living from this tasty and dangerous drug that temporarily blots out reality.

Per year the average German drinks:

140 litres (245 pints) of beer
27 litres (48 pints) of wine
7 litres (12 pints) of schnapps, cognac, whisky etc.

From the Brockhaus Encyclopedia, the German "Britannica":

Acute symptoms of drunkenness include intoxication and reduced muscle coordination and balance due to the narcotic effect of the alcohol on the central nervous system (unsteady gait), impairment of speech (mumbling), impairment of the central regulation of cutaneous vessel temperature, hallucinations (white mice → delirium tremens).

Cheers!

If any country apart from Japan and Korea gives the impression that its people *leben, um zu arbeiten* (= live to work), and don't *arbeiten, um zu leben* (= work to live), then it's Germany. But even if this is true, they still also like to party. Especially on Fridays or Saturdays because next day they can lie in – here things are the same all over the world.

If someone invites people privately to his or her home then it's either for a meal or a party. A small present for the host will not come amiss. Germans usually take a bottle of wine or champagne, but often a book or a CD. The hostess is often given a bouquet.

It's (almost) always interesting to be invited to a meal. You find out what people eat and have the opportunity to chat informally. Often other guests are invited too so that you meet new people. Many a marriage has resulted from such an invitation.

At a party it's noisier, and you are free to circulate, chatting to one person after another until you come across someone you find really interesting and perhaps attractive as well. The Germans tend to be a bit perfectionist about their parties. The cold buffet, the drinks, everything must be just right, as the hosts are anxious not to make a bad impression. Whether the party is really successful and entertaining, however, depends on the guests, the mood everyone is in, what people talk about and how stimulating the music is.

If you are going to go to a party, however, someone must first say to you: *Ich möchte Sie einladen* (= I'd like to invite you round/out).

Some people who have no time or inclination to organize their party themselves get a party service to do it for them. Food and drinks are then brought all ready prepared to the house. Someone who's really got a lot of money hires an entertainer or even a whole orchestra.

zu uns	to our place
die Party	party
die Leute	people
soll ich	should I
mitbringen	to bring
für alles gesorgt	everything taken care of
gegen neun	around nine
ich freue mich	I'm glad

Motion towards or in one position?

zu uns → to our place/house
bei uns → at our place/house

Instead of *die Party* the German word *das Fest* is also often used.

die Leute - this word is in the plural and there is no singular. There are also words that are only in the singular (*Wasser, Zucker*, etc.) In the dictionary there is then no plural ending.

sorgen is the verb (= to take care of), *gesorgt* is the past participle i.e. the work has already been done.

Ich möchte Sie zu uns einladen.	I would like to invite you to our place.
Ja?	Yes?
Ja. Wir geben morgen eine Party.	Yes. We're having a party tomorrow.
Sehr nett.	Very nice.
Es kommen viele interessante Leute.	A lot of interesting people are coming.
Soll ich etwas mitbringen?	Should I bring anything?
Nein danke, das ist nicht nötig. ..	No, thank you, that's not necessary.
Vielleicht etwas zu trinken?	Maybe something to drink?
Nein, wirklich nicht.	No, really not.
Gut.	Good.
Es ist für alles gesorgt.	Everything's taken care of.
Um wie viel Uhr soll ich kommen?	At what time shall I come?
So gegen neun.	Around nine.
Wunderbar, bis morgen.	Great, till tomorrow then.
Ich freue mich.	I'm glad you can come.

alles is a great deal of *etwas* and the opposite of ...? Correct, of *nichts*.

gegen halb neun means at approximately 8.30.

Ich freue mich – these verbs which have another pronoun in the same person are called reflexive verbs:
sich freuen
ich freue mich
er freut sich
sie freut sich
Sie freuen sich
wir freuen uns
Note: *er/sie/Sie* → *sich*

1. Ask if you can do something

You can do this exercise quite mechanically, but you can also try to imagine situations corresponding to each sentence.

Soll ich ***Ihnen die 100 Dollars wechseln?***
1. Ich wechsle Ihnen die 100 Dollars.
2. Ich rufe Sie heute Abend an.
3. Ich fahre für Sie nach Berlin.
4. Ich komme zu der Party mit.
5. Ich rate mal.
6. Ich nehme den Zug.
7. Ich vergesse das alles.
8. Ich trinke den Sherry alleine.
9. Ich glaube das wirklich.

2. Find the right question

Not every question is always right.

1. So gegen neun.
   - a ■ Um wie viel Uhr soll ich kommen?
   - b ■ Kommen Sie um neun?

2. Bei unseren Partys immer.
   - a ■ Kommen interessante Leute?
   - b ■ Um wie viel Uhr soll ich kommen?

3. Ja, sehr.
   - a ■ Gibt es etwas zu trinken?
   - b ■ Freuen Sie sich?

4. Ja, gerne.
   - a ■ Geben Sie eine Party?
   - b ■ Möchten Sie morgen zu uns kommen?

3. Have a guess

First decide what is meant and then look for the German word for it. You know all the words you're looking for.

1. What you add on top of the actual bill.
2. Typical German dish, not from Bavaria, not from Berlin.
3. It says what there is to satisfy your hunger.
4. An event everyone looks forward to.
5. This is what you are if you can't wait to find something out.

4. Sort into matching pairs

In life everything is somehow connected, but here there's one connection for each item.

1. der ICE
2. Lufthansa
3. der Bäcker
4. die Vorspeise
5. die Katastrophe

   - a ■ die Suppe
   - b ■ Pilz-Allergie
   - c ■ der Zug
   - d ■ das Vollkornbrot
   - e ■ die Fluglinie

herzlich willkommen	welcome
bei uns	at our place
reinkommen	to come in
doch	do please
klein	little, small
ablegen	take off (coat)
der Gast	guest
den ganzen Tag	all day
hinten	at the back
tanzen	dance

Herzlich willkommen bei uns.	It's nice to have you here.
Guten Abend.	Good evening.
Kommen Sie doch bitte rein.	Do come in.
Hier – ein kleines Geschenk.	I've brought you a little present.
Legen Sie ab.	Let me take your coat.
Bin ich der Erste?	Am I the first?
Nein, es sind schon andere Gäste da.	No there are other guests here already.
Hier in der Küche gibt es etwas zu essen.	There's something to eat here in the kitchen.
Mhhm. Ich habe schon den ganzen Tag Hunger.	Mmm. I've been hungry all day.
Und dort hinten...	And back there...
Ja?	Yes?
... dort können Sie tanzen.	... there you can dance.
Zuerst möchte ich aber etwas essen...	But first I would like something to eat.

herzlich willkommen bei uns – literally "a hearty welcome to our house" – always sounds full of feeling, arms open wide, a heartfelt welcome.

reinkommen and *hereinkommen* are the same thing and they're separable, too: *Ich komme rein. Kann ich hereinkommen?*

Doch is another one of those problematic German words: it can mean "but", "still", "after all", but here it's being used for emphasis and can best be rendered using the verb "to do".

klein is the opposite of *groß.* Both are good words to have handy, after all everything's relative and comparable. Well – almost everything.

Did you notice? *der Gast* – *die Gäste.* Some words change their root vowel in the plural:

der Mann	*die Männer*
der Ausgang	*die Ausgänge*
die Wurst	*die Würste*
der Pass	*die Pässe*
der Zug	*die Züge*

There's no hard-and-fast rule for this, but they are only words with an -a-, -o-, or -u-.

Ein kleines Geschenk is always a nice gesture, especially when the host has gone to such a lot of trouble. Some people have no time at all for the preparations, and have the food sent in. It's all a question of cost.

der ganze Tag	all day
die ganze Woche	all week
das ganze Jahr	all year

dort	there
dort hinten	back there

1. Put in the right order

When you put things in order, you are putting your knowledge of German syntax into practice.

1. uns - möchte - Sie - ich - einladen - zu
2. etwas - zuerst - essen - aber - ich - möchte
3. andere - da - schon - sind - Gäste - es
4. Leute - es - viele - interessante - kommen
5. es - alles - für - gesorgt - ist

2. What is it in English?

Translate this, and then you'll have a passive knowledge of the expressions. When you accept an invitation, make sure you're also able to use them.

1. den ganzen Tag _____
2. ein Geschenk mitbringen __
3. so gegen neun _____
4. ich freue mich _____
5. andere Gäste sind schon da _

6. kommen Sie rein _____
7. das ist nicht nötig _____
8. tanzen Sie _____
9. legen Sie ab _____
10. hinten in der Küche _____

3. Put these sentences in the plural

Here the plural involves a particular change.

Ich brauche die Pässe.
1. Ich brauche den Pass.
2. Wo ist der Ausgang?
3. Der Zug ist mir lieber.
4. Wir essen heute die Wurst.
5. Der Gast schläft heute hier.
6. Ich finde das Buch interessant.

4. Find the partners

They are not all opposites.

1. klein
2. sehen
3. zu Fuß
4. links
5. geben
6. auf keinen Fall

a ■ mit dem Auto
b ■ immer
c ■ nehmen
d ■ groß
e ■ hören
f ■ rechts

5. What's missing?

Don't look straight at the key, turn back a few pages.

1. Ich habe den _____ Tag nichts gegessen.
2. Kommen Sie doch bitte _____.
3. Ich möchte Sie zu unserer Party _____.
4. Es ist für _____ gesorgt.
5. Ich freue _____.

Every year in mid-September the mayor of Munich taps the first barrel of beer and opens yet another *Oktoberfest*. Beer drinking is the focal point of this huge festival, and to save the waiters' legs, the beer is dispensed in litre mugs. Even if you aren't a beer drinker you should still go, as where else can you see real Bavarians in leather shorts engaged in finger wrestling? There are major festivals elsewhere in Germany too, such as in Stuttgart, or in Cologne, Düsseldorf and Mainz in the Rhineland where the big carnival processions are held.

The most important festival for both the family and the retail trade is Christmas. On the evening of 24th December the whole family gathers round the Christmas tree, and might sing or put on a recording of Christmas carols; presents are exchanged and a special meal is eaten.

A week later it's New Year's Eve. From ten o'clock in the evening everyone (except the taxi drivers) is a bit tipsy, and, as at carnival, people can get a bit carried away. A man and woman can easily start flirting and forget that they are actually married to someone else.

While on the subject of flirting – German men are rather cautious and reserved, and the women are on their guard so as not to fall prey to a lady-killer. Although frank compliments are rather frowned on, women still rather like them – only of course when they come from a nice man.

Germany has 16 *Länder*, which to some extent have their own public holidays according to whether they are more Catholic or more Protestant. The following important public holidays are observed throughout Germany:

New Year ....01.01.
Good Friday
Easter Monday
Labour Day ....01.05.
Whit Monday
Ascension Day
Day of German Unity ...03.10.
Christmas ....25/26.12.

On all these days most people don't have to go to work, shops and banks etc. are all closed, and the bus and train timetables are different. Note that on the evening of 24 December everything comes to a standstill, there are no shops open, and it is even hard to find somewhere to go for a drink.

einhundertneun **109**

T Test 4

1. Which is right?

Don't think about the
exceptions, although of
course there are some.

früh is "early", *Stück* is
"piece" – so the word
breakfast means the first
bite early in the morning.

See the margin note on
number 1.

The author also likes sitting
in a café and having a good
conversation. Unfortunately
this is not possible every day.

What is meant is what the
Germans do in their free
time.

Imagine yourself with a
Maß Bier.
How many could you
drink?

1. *Frühstück* for the Germans is
    a ■ rather important.
    b ■ rather unimportant.
    c ■ neither nor.
2. *Arbeitsfrühstück* is a breakfast
    a ■ after finishing work.
    b ■ before starting work.
    c ■ with business partners.
3. Men diet and do keep-fit exercises in order to pursue
    a ■ their idea of the perfect body.
    b ■ wild animals.
    c ■ other men.
4. There have been cafés in Europe since the
    a ■ 2nd century BC.
    b ■ 17th century AD.
    c ■ 19th century AD.
5. When people get together in the evenings they generally
    a ■ also meet to grumble.
    b ■ also dance.
    c ■ also drink.
6. At the *Oktoberfest* the beer is served
    a ■ in half litre mugs.
    b ■ in litre mugs.
    c ■ in two-litre mugs.

2. Answers and questions

Take care not to mix up
a and **d**.

1. Sonst noch was?
2. Kommen Sie mit?
3. Hier – ein Geschenk für Sie.
4. Was darf ich Ihnen bringen?
5. Kann ich zahlen bitte?
6. Soll ich etwas mitbringen?

a ■ Danke, das ist aber nicht nötig.
b ■ Sauerkraut bitte.
c ■ Ich komme sofort.
d ■ Nein, das ist wirklich nicht nötig.
e ■ Ja, bitte ein Ei.
f ■ Gern, vielleicht ins Café?

3. Multiple choice

1. Wir _____ morgen eine Party.
   - a ■ geben
   - b ■ nehmen
   - c ■ kommen

2. Kommen Sie bitte so _____ neun.
   - a ■ am
   - b ■ für
   - c ■ gegen

3. Ich _____ gerne noch eine Tasse Kaffee.
   - a ■ hatte
   - b ■ hätte
   - c ■ haben

4. Wir _____ mit dem Auto fahren.
   - a ■ kommen
   - b ■ können
   - c ■ möchte

5. Was _____ Sie zu essen?
   - a ■ es gibt
   - b ■ wünschen
   - c ■ heißen

6. Es kommen viele _____ Leute.
   - a ■ interessante
   - b ■ interaktiven
   - c ■ interessanten

This sort of exercise is stress because you have to take a decision, and only one answer is possible in each case.

With number 2 it is a question of the meaning: around 9 o'clock. In German *um neun Uhr,* is also possible, meaning punctually at nine.

4. Sense and nonsense

1. Are you paying with (fried) sausage?
2. Other braised beefs are already here.
3. We are boiling a party tomorrow.
4. I have already had starters all day.
5. Have you got a party allergy?
6. I would like to forget you.

The author has to admit that he had great fun writing this exercise. One of the sentences, by the way might well be useful in life, especially after a separation.

17 A normal family?

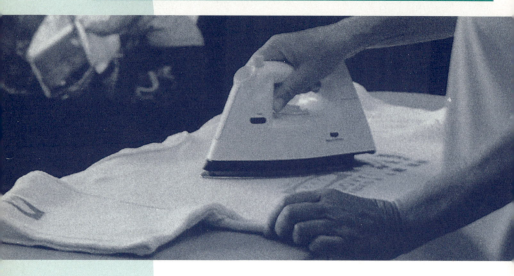

Die Lindenstraße

is the name of the most popular German TV series. It has been running non-stop since the early 80s, and has long passed its 600th episode. The success of *Die Lindenstraße* is perhaps due to the fact that every single viewer can find someone to identify with: foreigners, gays, blacks, fascists, antifascists, criminals and worthy citizens, this national soap opera has them all.

Gerda Schwarz is a housewife. In the morning she gets up and makes breakfast for her family. When her husband and children have gone she does her housework. This takes about an hour. Then she lights a cigarette and sits down in front of the television. With the remote control she hops from one channel to the next to see if she can find a soap opera. That's something you can get involved in, sharing the fears, romantic feelings, problems and joys of the characters. You know the people, know who's bad and who's good, and it's exciting because something's always happening.

At eleven Gerda goes shopping. When she comes back, she reaches for the remote control again and switches to a nice chat show.

When the children come home from school, they eat, have a rest and then there's homework to do. Gerda might do the ironing then – preferably in front of the television. Later on the children also want to watch a bit of television, preferably pop videos.

When Mr Schwarz comes home in the evening, the television's on and the family have their evening meal. Afterwards they move over to the armchairs in the living room. There are often arguments about what programme to watch, especially with the children. There's only one thing for it: the children will have to have their own television.

Is the Schwarz family an extreme case? Not at all, this is an international phenomenon.

liebe	dear
der Zuschauer	viewer
besonders	particularly
vorstellen	to introduce
kennen	to know
ihn	him
das Fernsehen	television
die Presse	press
der Musiker	musician
der Filmschauspieler	film actor
der Olympiasieger	Olympic gold-medallist
meine Damen und Herren	ladies and gentlemen

Liebe Zuschauer, (= Dear viewers) is plural. The singular is *lieb-er Zuschauer*
lieb-e Zuschauerin

Liebe / lieber is what you also write at the beginning of a letter, to friends, to family members and people you already know.

„Liebe Zuschauer
ich darf Ihnen heute
einen besonders interessanten
Gast vorstellen.
Viele kennen ihn
aus dem Fernsehen
und aus der Presse.
Er ist Musiker und Student,
Ingenieur und Journalist,
Filmschauspieler
und Olympiasieger,
meine Damen und Herren,
heute bei uns:
S U P E R M A N N!"

"(Dear viewers)
Today I would like
to present to you a
particularly interesting guest.
Many will know him
from television
and the press.
He's a musician and a student,
an engineer and a journalist,
film actor
and Olympic gold-medallist,
ladies and gentlemen,
with us today:
S U P E R M A N!"

If *interessant* is not sufficient, then you say *sehr interessant;* if that is still not enough, then *besonders interessant.*

Accusative pronouns

Sie kennen	*mich (ich)*
ich kenne	*Sie (Sie)*
ich kenne	*ihn (er)*
ich kenne	*sie (sie)*
Sie kennen	*uns (wir)*

The accusative comes for example after: *kennen, brauchen, einladen, finden, sehen, vergessen…*

1. Introduce someone

Ihnen is the dative, *meine Frau* is the accusative. Don't forget, when there's an accusative, the masculine *mein* becomes *meinen*, and *der* becomes *den*.

*Darf ich Ihnen **meine Frau** vorstellen?*
1. meine Frau
2. mein Mann
3. mein Freund Georg Jacobi
4. meine Freundin Claire Wilberg aus London
5. der Musiker Hans Werner Henze
6. der Ingenieur Dr. Jochen Hucke
7. mein Professor
8. meine Freundin
9. der Filmschauspieler Dustin Hofmann

2. Put them together

c and **e** are interchangeable from the point of view of grammar, but not of content.

1. Ich kenne Boris Becker   a ■ mich nicht.
2. Ludwig van Beethoven war   b ■ vorstellen.
3. Ich möchte Ihnen meinen Mann   c ■ Filmschauspieler.
4. Viele kennen   d ■ aus der Presse.
5. Götz George ist ein deutscher   e ■ Musiker.

3. Find the right pronoun:
mich, ihn, sie, Sie, uns

Not to be confused: *Sie* is the form of address, *sie* is the third person "she" (Petra or Frau Krug). If you are uncertain, turn back to the previous page where the corresponding pronouns are given in the margin.

1. Ich kenne _____. (er)
2. Wir möchten _____ etwas fragen. (Sie)
3. Können Sie _____ zurückrufen? (wir)
4. Meine Frau braucht _____. (ich)
5. Ich kann _____ nicht sehen. (er)
6. Er hat _____ eingeladen. (Sie)
7. Vergessen Sie _____! (ich)
8. Kennen Sie _____? (sie)
9. Haben Sie _____ angerufen? (wir)

4. Fruit salad

Note that in the 4th sentence *auch* does not come in second place, as in English.
No. 5 is a question, so the first word is already in the right place.

1. Ihnen - einen interessanten - ich - darf - Gast - vorstellen _____
2. eine Suppe - Petra - möchte - kochen - uns _____
3. Maria - sehr nett - mich - findet _____
4. finde - sie -ich - besonders nett - auch _____
5. darf - einladen?- ich - zu einem Wein - Sie _____

Guten Abend	Good evening
die Nachrichten	news
der Papst	Pope
zurückkommen	to come back
der Bundeskanzler	(Federal) Chancellor
der Bürgermeister	mayor
zusammenkommen	to meet
gesprochen	talked
der Bundesfinanzminister	(Federal) Minister of Finance
mitteilen	to announce
dass	that
die Regierung	government

Guten Abend,
meine Damen und Herren,
Hier die Nachrichten.
Rom:
Der Papst ist heute von einer Reise
nach Amerika zurückgekommen.
Berlin:
Der Bundeskanzler ist heute
mit dem Bürgermeister
zusammengekommen.
Sie haben über die
Probleme von Berlin gesprochen.
Bonn:
Der Bundesfinanzminister
hat heute mitgeteilt,
dass die Regierung ab
sofort kein Geld mehr hat.

Good evening,
ladies and gentlemen,
here is the news.
Rome:
Today the Pope came
back from a visit to America.
Berlin:
The Federal Chancellor today
met the mayor.

They talked about Berlin's
problems.
Bonn:
The Federal Minister of
Finance announced today
that the government no
longer has any money.

Nachrichten
The news is broadcast hourly on the radio and several times a day on television. The most popular news broadcasts are those on Channel 1: the *Tagesschau* and late in the evening the *Tagesthemen*.

gesprochen comes from *sprechen*. *Sprechen mit…* is used for a person, *sprechen über* for the subject that is being talked about.

The negative form *nicht mehr*
Schlafen Sie noch? – Nein, ich schlafe nicht mehr. = Are you still asleep? No I'm not asleep any more.
Haben Sie noch Geld? – Nein, ich habe kein Geld mehr. = Do you have any money left? No, I don't have any more money / any money left.
In English there are many ways of rendering *noch*, depending on the context.

The past participle of separable verbs

einkaufen	eingekauft
mitteilen	mitgeteilt
anrufen	angerufen
einladen	eingeladen
mitkommen	mitgekommen
wegfahren	weggefahren
zurückkommen	zurückgekommen
zurückrufen	zurückgerufen

A German problem
Subordinate clauses (for example those introduced with *dass*) must always have the verb right at the end. This is just one of those things. And it is also impractical – you always have to wait such a long time before you discover what the sentence is about:
Der Bundeskanzler hat gesagt, dass er heute in Berlin auf dem Alexander-Platz um neun Uhr ein Bier trinkt.

2/33

1. Have you got any dollars left?

> Sentences 7 to 9: The opposite of *etwas* or *alles* is *nichts*.

*Nein, ich habe **keine Dollars** mehr.*

1. Haben Sie noch Dollars?
2. Bekommen Sie noch ein Bier?
3. Möchten Sie noch eine Pizza?
4. Brauchen Sie noch Reisechecks?
5. Haben Sie noch eine Kreditkarte?
6. Schulden Sie mir noch Geld?
7. Wünschen Sie noch etwas?
8. Verstehen Sie noch alles?
9. Bringen Sie morgen noch etwas mit?

2. Give the German for the following…

> *Bundesfinanzminister* is another one of those German words that go on for ever. They are always deciphered working backwards from the end of the word: it's the minister who allocates the finances of the Federation.

1. The Federal Chancellor ___
2. The mayor _____
3. The viewer _____
4. Television _____
5. The Federal Minister of Finance _____
6. The press _____

3. Are you still working?

> This exercise is similar to the first one, but this time it is not nouns but verbs that are being put in the negative form with *nicht*.

*Nein, ich **arbeite** nicht mehr.*

1. Arbeiten Sie noch?
2. Kaufen Sie heute noch ein?
3. Glauben Sie das immer noch?
4. Finden Sie ihn noch nett?
5. Zahlen Sie noch heute?
6. Bleiben Sie noch?
7. Fahren Sie noch nach München?
8. Leben Sie noch?

4. Put in the past tense

2/34

> A repetition of something you already know: verbs expressing motion take *sein* in the perfect, while the others take *haben*.

*Herr Carls **ist** heute nicht **zurückgekommen**.*

1. Herr Carls kommt heute nicht zurück.
2. Peter Urban fährt nicht weg.
3. Hans Meisner ruft nicht an.
4. Georg Biesalski lädt uns ein.
5. Ursula Steffens ruft nicht zurück.
6. Wir fahren weg.
7. Marta Greisel kauft ein.
8. Theo Storch kommt gerne mit.
9. Jürgen Frank ruft sofort zurück.

5. Fill in the gaps

> If someone embarks on a career in German television as a result of this exercise and becomes a newsreader or presenter, please tell the publisher.

1. Der erste Mann in der Regierung ist der _ _ _ _ _ _ _ _ _ _ _ _ _.
2. Der Bürgermeister ist von einer Reise _ _ _ _ _ _ _ _ _ _ _ _ _ _ _.
3. Zeitungen, Bücher… das zusammen ist nicht das Fernsehen, das ist die _ _ _ _ _ _.
4. Eine gute Nachricht: der Bundesfinanzminister hat _ _ _ _ _ _ _ _ _ _, dass die Regierung wieder Geld hat.
5. Robert de Niro ist kein Musiker, er ist _ _ _ _ _ _ _ _ _ _ _ _ _ _ _.
6. „Liebe _ _ _ _ _ _ _ _ _, heute bei uns im Fernsehen: der Bundeskanzler von Österreich!"

Perhaps German television is better than the reputation that it has amongst Germans. Channel 1 is a public broadcasting station that broadcasts on a regional basis in the early evening; Channel 2, ZDF, is the largest broadcasting company in Europe, and there are twelve regional third channels, which together make up Channel 1 and also produce high-quality educational television independently as Channel 3. The commercial stations make no attempt to compete with the public ones as far as quality is concerned, but have large audiences. The viewing figures are the sword of Damocles hanging over good television: the more viewers, the more income from advertising, it's as simple as that. Advertisements are still only allowed in the early evening on the public channels. And a 90-minute film on a commercial channel still lasts a full two hours (This is something of a problem for the waterworks, since when the adverts come on there's a rush for the toilet and a considerable drop in pressure in the water pipes as a result). At a time when it is being lamented that people lead increasingly isolated lives and don't communicate, talkshows are very successful. As happens all over the world, famous people are asked about their lives and profit from the free advertising because they are once again in the limelight. Some discussions are so organized that the sparks are guaranteed to fly: invite a conservative bishop and a feminist supporter of abortion and you can be sure the programme will not be boring.

The public TV stations

ARD
(7 regional stations) Channel 1
ZDF (Mainz)   Channel 2
plus eleven regional
3rd channels
SF Schweizer Fernsehen
Swiss Television
ORF1, ORF2
Österreichischer Rundfunk
Austrian Broadcasting
Corporation

Private TV stations

RTL (Cologne)
Sat 1 (Mainz)
Pro 7 (Munich)
Vox (Cologne)

The cultural stations

3 Sat (ARD, ZDF, Switzerland
and Austria)
Arte (ARD/ZDF and France)

Arte in particular is a model of good television. Amongst its best features are the evenings devoted to a single topic, which is presented with a feature film, a documentary and a discussion amongst experts.

Something has changed in society. In the year 1900 just 7.5 % of households were single households. If today the percentage is 50, what will it be in the year 2050?

Some singles do not want to commit themselves and prefer to keep changing their partners. Others are living alone against their will. And yet others would be living alone if it were not more comfortable at home. It is not unusual to find unmarried 30-year-olds with regular jobs still living with their mothers because the rent is cheaper, their washing is done and their food is put on the table.

Elvira Knoll works behind the service counter at a bank. At 31 she's living alone and finds this "quite normal". So it is, as over half the households in Germany are single households. Sometimes Elvira is not sure whether it might not be nicer to live with a partner.

But it is not so easy to find "the right one". In the bank all her colleagues already have partners, and none of the customers are of interest either. She has tried out a number of things: she has answered newspaper advertisements, she's been to organized singles parties, and once she was even in a show on television. There she sat with two other women behind a partition and an unknown man put previously arranged questions. He found Elvira the nicest and they won a weekend away together, but that was rather boring, apart from the photographer who followed them around all the time taking photos for television.

Elvira has also had two longer relationships, but never actually lived with the men concerned. In both cases it was all over after six months.

Now she has become a bit more cautious when a man says to her: *Haben Sie Zeit? Ich möchte Sie gerne einladen* (= Are you free? I would like to invite you out).

fragen	to ask
die Zeit	time
wofür	for what
wozu	to what
das Kino	cinema
ich mag	I like
mögen	to like
der Film	film
das Theater	theatre
die Disko	disco

mögen

ich mag
Sie mögen
er/sie mag
wir mögen

Möchten Sie ...? comes from *mögen.* It's not necessary for you to know that it is the imperfect subjunctive.

Entschuldigung?	Excuse me?
Ja, bitte?	Yes?
Mein Name ist Daniels.	My name is Daniels.
Ja?	Yes?
Darf ich Sie etwas fragen?	May I ask you something?
Ja bitte.	Yes.
Haben Sie vielleicht morgen Zeit?	Do you maybe have any time tomorrow?
Zeit wofür?	Time for what?
Ich möchte Sie gerne einladen.	I would like to invite you out.
Einladen wozu?	Invite me to what?
Vielleicht ins Kino?	Perhaps to the cinema?
Ich mag keine Filme.	I don't like films.
Dann vielleicht ins Theater?	Then perhaps to the theatre?
Theater mag ich auch nicht.	I don't like the theatre either.
Ja... vielleicht in die Disko?	Well... perhaps to a disco?
Schön ... ich tanze gerne.	Great ... I like dancing.
Wunderbar, morgen um neun, ist das Okay?	Wonderful, tomorrow around nine, is that okay?

in das → *ins*

ins Kino, ins Theater, ins Hotel, ins Auto, ins Reisebüro, ins Fernsehen, ins Flugzeug, etc. – but only when movement is involved, i.e. after verbs such as *gehen, fahren* ... And only with neuter words (ones that have the article *das*). Otherwise it's *in die Disko* and *in den Zug (der Zug).*

wofür, because *Zeit für* is implied
wozu, because *einladen zu* is implied

For a change an exercise you can do automatically, without having to think about it. It's a way of engraving the expression concerned on your mind.

1. I don't like it/them either

*Ich mag **auch** keine Filme.*

1. Ich mag keine Filme.
2. Ich mag keine Zeitungen.
3. Ich mag keine Bratwurst.
4. Ich mag kein Bier.
5. Ich mag keine Zuschauer.
6. Ich mag keine Bahnhöfe.
7. Ich mag keinen Sauerbraten.
8. Ich mag keine Bundeskanzler.
9. Ich mag keine Rechnungen.
10. Ich mag keine Verspätungen.

You know this exercise. Whether you also like it is another matter.

2. Which answer is right?

1. Haben Sie morgen Zeit?
   - a ■ Leider nicht.
   - b ■ Ich frühstücke nicht.
2. Tanzen Sie gerne?
   - a ■ Ja, ich tanze nicht gerne.
   - b ■ Nein, ich mag keine Diskos.
3. Mögen Sie Bahnhöfe?
   - a ■ Nein, ich reise nicht gerne.
   - b ■ Nein, ich mag keine Hotels.
4. Darf ich Sie etwas fragen?
   - a ■ Was möchten Sie wissen?
   - b ■ Ich habe eine Frage.
5. Haben Sie über Probleme gesprochen?
   - a ■ Ja, wir haben über alles gesprochen.
   - b ■ Nein, wir sprechen über Probleme.

The first sentence is a polite way of inviting someone out, but no. 9 is a bit bold and no. 10 pretty unimaginative. Even so, it's better than "Would you like to see my etchings?"

3. The first approach

*Haben Sie Zeit, darf ich Sie **ins Kino** einladen?*

1. ins Kino
2. ins Theater
3. in die Disko
4. ins Restaurant
5. zum Frühstück
6. nach Acapulco
7. zu einer Party
8. ins Café
9. ins Hotel
10. zum Fernsehen

Here *mag* is used with a noun, *gerne* with a verb. *Mag* can also be used with a verb: *Ich mag jetzt nicht sprechen.*

4. Form sentences

*Ich mag **keine Restaurants**, ich **esse** nicht gerne.*

1. Restaurants / essen
2. Telefone / anrufen
3. Rotwein / trinken
4. Probleme / reden
5. Parties / tanzen
6. Urlaub / reisen
7. Supermärkte / einkaufen
8. Diskos / tanzen

getrennt	separated
es ist aus	it's all over
man	you, one
sich trennen	to separate
eigentlich schon	in fact
lieben	to be in love with, love
der Rechtsanwalt	lawyer
sagen	to say
sich scheiden lassen	to get divorced
wir lassen uns scheiden	we're getting divorced
die Kinder	children

man

This is always used when something general is being expressed and it is not important who the subject of an action is. *Man arbeitet von 8 bis 17 Uhr.* – It's obvious that this does not refer to the unemployed but the working population.

eigentlich is a another hard word to translate, meaning "in fact", "really", and when combined with *schon* would be emphasized in English with an additional verb, as here: "… we did in fact."

sagen

ich sage
Sie sagen
er/sie sagt
wir sagen
past participle: *gesagt*

sich scheiden lassen is a complicated construction. It is reflexive like *sich freuen*, and is also accompanied by a verb that functions like *dürfen* und *können,* and is therefore always followed by the infinitive.
ich lasse mich scheiden
Sie lassen sich scheiden
er lässt sich scheiden
wir lassen uns scheiden

ich liebe dich – many know this sentence in German even though they don't speak German at all. But we won't be learning the sentence in this book, because we are concentrating on the polite form of address *Sie*. Family members, friends and young people use *du*, which is where *dich* comes from.

Und wie geht es Ihrer Frau?	And how is your wife?
Ich weiß es nicht.	I don't know.
Sie wissen es nicht?	You don't know?
Nein – wir haben uns getrennt.	No – we've separated.
Was?	What?
Ja, es ist aus.	Yes, it's all over.
Man kann sich doch nicht trennen … einfach so.	But you can't separate … just like that.
Nein, natürlich nicht.	No, of course not.
Hatten Sie Probleme?	Did you have problems?
Ja, eigentlich schon.	Yes, we did in fact.
Große Probleme?	Big problems?
Ja, meine Frau liebt einen anderen.	Yes, my wife's in love with someone else.
Au, au, au…	Oh dear, oh dear.
Ich war schon beim Rechtsanwalt.	I've already seen a lawyer.
Und was hat er gesagt?	And what did he say?
Na, ja, wir lassen uns scheiden.	Well, we're getting divorced.
Und die Kinder…?	And what about the children…?

Sentences 2 and 5 both have two possible answers.

1. Form correct sentences

1.	Haben Sie vielleicht	a ■	ins Kino einladen.
2.	Darf ich Sie	b ■	kein Theater.
3.	Es ist aus, wir lassen	c ■	etwas fragen?
4.	Ich mag leider	d ■	heute Abend Zeit?
5.	Ich möchte Sie gerne	e ■	uns scheiden.

This translation is a bit more complicated, but you will find all the sentences on page 119 or 121.

2. Translate into German

1. I don't like dancing.
2. I have no time.
3. We're getting divorced.
4. Have you seen a lawyer?
5. We've separated.
6. What did he say?
7. May I ask you something?
8. My wife's in love with someone else.

The last sentence is a bit odd, but there are situations in life when you forget yourself.

3. Put in the first person

Ich freue mich.
1. Wir freuen uns.
2. Wir trennen uns.
3. Wir lassen uns scheiden.
4. Wir sehen uns.
5. Wir vergessen uns.

Apart from the additional *nicht* in the last sentence, it should all be quite simple.

4. Say that something can't be done

*Man kann **sich** doch nicht **trennen**, einfach so.*
1. sich trennen
2. im Restaurant tanzen
3. beim Bundeskanzler anrufen
4. Wasser essen
5. im Urlaub arbeiten
6. sieben Rotwein trinken
7. zu Fuß nach Spanien gehen
8. die Rechnung nicht bezahlen

Partnership is a constant topic of conversation among Germans. The newspapers, too, are full of it, the bookshops have shelves of books giving advice, there are public discussions on the radio and television, and if the tables in the cafés could talk, they would have an awful lot to tell.

Marriage is considered a natural state of affairs, but it has been adapting to changing social conditions. Today the main point of it is no longer a family with children – many marriages remain deliberately childless. In the course of the student movement of 1968, marriage itself was also questioned and other forms of living together were tried out, such as communal living. Living together without being married has remained with us and is no problem at all nowadays: it only becomes difficult when children or an inheritance are involved. In the meantime, the conservative institution of marriage is experiencing a revival, and weddings are again becoming more traditional, with the bride in white and the ceremony held in church.

Overall, however, marriage has shifted noticeably in the direction of a partnership. The economic dependence of women on their husbands has greatly decreased, as many women earn their own money, and the women's movement has been at least partly responsible for the fact that men today do more in the home and are not so macho as they were perhaps around 30 years ago. But marriage is still in a state of crisis – every third one does not survive in the long term and ends in divorce.

It is now also acceptable for homosexual couples to live together. Some are also fighting for legal recognition, but marriage for homosexuals is not yet in sight.

It sounds good, what the women's movement is said to have achieved. But most women still complain that the men do too little, don't take the rubbish out often enough, almost never do the ironing, hardly ever go shopping, and still feel that men could in general do a bit more in the shared home.

From head to foot (or the other way round)

Some important parts of the body

der Fuß	foot
das Bein	leg
der Po	bottom
der Bauch	stomach
der Rücken	back
die Brust	chest, breast
der Busen	breasts
die Schulter	shoulder
der Arm	arm
die Hand	hand
der Finger	finger
der Hals	neck
das Gesicht	face
der Mund	mouth
das Ohr	ear
die Nase	nose
das Auge	eye
der Kopf	head

Christa Schneider is not feeling well this morning. When she woke up, she felt as if her head was in a vice, and when she tried to get out of bed, her legs gave way. And when she eventually made it to the bathroom and was peering at herself in the mirror, she suddenly felt a stabbing pain in her back as if she was getting 20 injections from the doctor at once. "That serves me right," she thinks, "that's what happens when you've overdone it the night before."

Health also has something to do with the sort of life we lead. Anyone not keeping to a balanced diet or getting enough exercise shouldn't be surprised when aches and pains set in later on in life. And we now know how seriously emotional problems can affect physical health. But what use is the knowledge that work and the climate in the office are making you ill when there is no alternative? In Germany people work hard and this is reflected in the nation's health: circulatory diseases are more frequent than in most other countries. Stomach problems on the other hand are a typical "foreigner's disease". This may be because foreigners have to swallow so much and can't defend themselves properly.

But one thing is clear: anyone, whether German or foreigner, who says *Alles tut mir weh* (= Everything hurts) and is told *Dann müssen Sie zum Arzt* (= Then you must go to the doctor), is not to be envied.

still	....	quiet
die Schmerzen	....	pains
der Kopf	....	head
wehtun	....	to ache
die Kopfschmerzen	....	headache
der Bauch	....	stomach
die Bauchschmerzen	....	stomach-ache
der Rücken	....	back
die Rückenschmerzen	....	backache
überall	....	everywhere
müssen	....	must

In German *die Schmerzen*, the plural form, is used more often than the singular, *der Schmerz.*

Instead of *der Kopf tut mir weh* you will often hear *mir tut der Kopf weh.* *Wehtun*, incidentally, is separable, i.e. *weh* normally comes at the end of the sentence.

As in English, there are two ways of saying that you have a pain:
1. *Der Bauch tut mir weh.* My stomach hurts.
2. *Ich habe Bauchschmerzen.* I've got stomach-ache.

Frau Schneider?	....	Frau Schneider?
Ja?	....	Yes?
Sie sind so still.	....	You're very quiet
...Ehemm...	....	Ermm...
Ist alles in Ordnung?	....	Is everything okay?
... ja ...	....	... yes ...
Sind Sie vielleicht krank?	....	Are you maybe ill?
Vielleicht ein bisschen...	....	I may be a bit...
Haben Sie Schmerzen?	....	Are you in pain?
Ja, der Kopf tut mir weh.	....	Yes, my head aches.
Aha ... Kopfschmerzen.	....	Aha ... a headache.
Ja, und der Bauch tut mir auch weh.	....	Yes and I've got stomach-ache too.
So? Bauchschmerzen!	....	Really? Stomach-ache!
Und der Rücken auch.	....	And backache, too.
Klar! Rückenschmerzen.	......	Of course! Backache.
Alles tut mir weh.	....	Everything hurts.
Sie sagen, Sie haben überall Schmerzen?	....	You say you've got pains everywhere?
Ja, überall.	....	Yes, everywhere.
Dann müssen Sie zum Arzt!	....	Then you must go to the doctor!

Not everyone is like Mrs Schneider. Some people just can't keep their aches and pains to themselves.

Actually it's *Sie müssen zum Arzt* **gehen.** But in colloquial German the verb is usually omitted with *müssen*. Everyone understands what's meant. When someone says *Ich muss nach Berlin* – then of course it means *mit dem Auto/Bus/Zug... fahren* or *mit dem Flugzeug fliegen* – it would be a bit too far to go there *zu Fuß* (= on foot).

1. Put it a different way

*Mir tut **der Kopf** weh.*
1. Ich habe Kopfschmerzen.
2. Ich habe Bauchschmerzen.
3. Ich habe Rückenschmerzen.
4. Ich habe Fußschmerzen.
5. Ich habe Weltschmerz.

Select from a-d one answer for each of the sentences on the left. Three answers theoretically go with sentence 1, so look for the answer to this one last.

2. Find the partners

1. Ist alles in Ordnung?
2. Sind Sie krank?
3. Sie sind so still!
4. Sie müssen zum Arzt.

a ■ Was soll ich sagen?
b ■ Ich mag keine Ärzte.
c ■ Nein. Ich glaube, ich bin krank.
d ■ Ja, mir tut alles weh.

Remember, only one solution fits.

3. What's missing?

1. Mir tut der Kopf _____.
   a ■ Schmerzen
   b ■ weh
   c ■ überall

2. Sie müssen unbedingt zum _____.
   a ■ gehen
   b ■ der Arzt
   c ■ Arzt

3. Alles _____ mir weh.
   a ■ gut
   b ■ tut
   c ■ Leid

4. Say what you must do

*Ja, ich muss **zum Arzt** gehen.*
1. Gehen Sie zum Arzt?
2. Fahren Sie morgen weg?
3. Arbeiten Sie heute?
4. Finden Sie das Problem?
5. Wechseln Sie Geld?
6. Rufen Sie unbedingt an?

This exercise may seem simple, but it will give you some useful sentences. That's what language learning is all about: diligence pays dividends.

5. Asking for something at the chemist's

*Ich brauche etwas gegen **Rückenschmerzen**.*
1. Rückenschmerzen
2. Kopfschmerzen
3. Fußschmerzen
4. Bauchschmerzen
5. Halsschmerzen

These sentences will only help you get pain-killers at the chemist's. If you are more seriously ill, then you will have to go to the doctor.

der Termin	appointment	schon einmal	before, already
ausfüllen	to fill in	das Formular	form
der Nächste	next	wo fehlt es denn?	what seems to be the matter?
das Fieber	temperature		
rauchen	to smoke	falsch	wrong
die Zigarette	cigarette	es gab	there was
der Kater	hangover		

Forms are something you will encounter in every bureaucratic situation. It is best to learn certain numbers off by heart: your passport number, your account number and the pin number for your bank card.

Guten Tag, mein Name ist Schneider. — Good morning, my name is Schneider.
Guten Tag. — Good morning.
Ich habe einen Termin um 10 Uhr 30. — I have an appointment at 10.30.
Waren Sie schon einmal hier? — Have you been here before?
Nein, noch nicht. — No, I haven't.
Dann füllen Sie bitte dieses Formular aus. — Then would you please fill in this form.
Ja. — Yes.
Und nehmen Sie dann bitte Platz. — And then take a seat.

Der Nächste, bitte. — *Next, please.*

Der Nächste bitte – you will often hear this at the doctor's, in the offices of public authorities, in shops and anywhere where people wait their turn and are called in one by one. When the doctor is short of time, he speaks into a microphone and you can hear him in the waiting room. Modern doctors, however, go personally to the waiting room to ask their patients to come into the consulting room.

Guten Tag, ...Frau Schneider. — Good morning, ...Mrs Schneider.
Guten Tag, Herr Doktor. — Good morning, doctor.
Wo fehlt's denn? — What seems to be the matter?
Ich habe Schmerzen. — I've got pains.
Wo? — Where?
Überall, der Kopf, der Bauch, der Rücken... — Everywhere, in my head, stomach, back...
Haben Sie Fieber? — Have you got a temperature?
Nein, ich glaube nicht. — No, I don't think so.
Haben Sie etwas Falsches gegessen? — Have you eaten something that wasn't OK?
Vielleicht, wir waren gestern eingeladen. — Perhaps, we were invited out yesterday.
Haben Sie viel geraucht? — Did you smoke a lot?
Es geht – so 20 oder 30 Zigaretten. — Not really – around 20 or 30 cigarettes.
Und haben Sie getrunken? — And did you drink?
Ja, ich weiß aber nicht mehr wie viel. — Yes, but I don't remember how much.
So, so... — Well, well...
Es gab Cocktails und Wein, und Kognak. — There were cocktails and wine and cognac.

Oh, oh – ganz einfach:
Sie haben einen Kater. — Oh – then it's quite simple: You've got a hangover.

Germans have a small plastic card from their health insurance company which is used to facilitate payment of medical costs. A sign of how computerized medicine has become. Whether this is always a good thing is another matter.

The doctor's diagnosis is not very medical, but it's very human ...
Mrs Schneider is an exception, she seems to be honest and is admitting that she's had a night of it. There is perhaps one sentence she still needs to say: *Nie wieder rauchen, nie wieder trinken!*
(= I'll never smoke again, I'll never drink again!)

1. *Wo fehlt's denn?*

2/44

Ich habe **Fieber**.
1. Fieber
2. Kopfschmerzen
3. zu viel geraucht
4. gestern Abend getrunken
5. vielleicht einen Kater
6. der Bauch tut weh

Another rather simple exercise, but one which will help you remember useful sentences. You can also amuse yourself imagining the situation in which you would use such a sentence.

2. Put in the correct order

Sort out the muddle. The question marks of course always come at the end. This is important, as whether or not the sentence is a question determines where the subject comes.

1. mir - weh - alles - tut _____
2. einmal - waren - schon - hier? - Sie _____
3. zu viel - habe - ich - getrunken - gestern _____
4. etwas - haben - Sie - gegessen? - Falsches _____

3. How does the sentence continue?

Only one solution is possible.

1. Ich habe 20 Zigaretten   a ■ Formular aus.
2. Waren Sie schon   b ■ sechzehn Uhr.
3. Füllen Sie bitte dieses   c ■ geraucht.
4. Sie haben getrunken, Sie   d ■ einmal hier?
5. Ich habe einen Termin um   e ■ haben einen Kater.

4. Put in the past tense

2/45

The fifth sentence sounds good, especially when you're hungry. The sixth sentence is a conversation stopper. This too happens in real life. But usually it's the person in the stronger position who says this.

Ich **habe** *vierzig Zigaretten* **geraucht**.
1. Ich rauche vierzig Zigaretten.
2. Ich trinke zwei Flaschen Kognak.
3. Ich esse drei Pizzas.
4. Ich arbeite 25 Stunden am Tag.
5. Ich koche Chinesisch.
6. Ich sage alles.

5. Long words to translate

The article (*der, die*) is always determined by the last word: *der Champignon*, but *die Suppe*.

1. der Sauerbraten _____
2. der Olympiasieger _____
3. die Rechtsanwälte _____
4. der Filmschauspieler _____
5. die Champignoncremesuppe _____
6. der Bundesfinanzminister _____

The Federal Republic is proud of its welfare state, which is supposed to function as a safety net. Unfortunately, more and more people are falling through it. There is talk of a new poverty affecting all age groups: young people with no prospects of getting a job; older people who are given notice as firms everywhere downsize, and old people whose pensions are just not enough to live on. In West Germany it is widows who have never worked who are particularly affected.

The state pension funds are gradually running out of money, as are the health insurance companies. And it's the ordinary people who feel this most. Glasses, false teeth, spa cures and certain types of treatment, which were automatically paid for years ago, are now no longer covered, or only in special circumstances. Preventive measures in particular have been drastically cut: although yoga, tai-chi or keep-fit courses are known to be beneficial, there's no money for them any more. For decades, wages were paid for six weeks in the case of illness. Now this principle is under threat, and it's being suggested that if a person is ill, part of his or her holiday should be forfeited. It is not hard to imagine the reaction of employees and unions to this.

The period of general prosperity seems to be coming to an end. Everyone is talking about globalization, and one of the global trends also affecting Germany, Austria and Switzerland is the tendency for the rich to get richer and the poor poorer.

Everything has its price

In the German economy the high *Lohnnebenkosten*, i.e. the subsidiary cost to the employer of the employee's pension and health insurance contributions in addition to his wages, are a major problem, as they can amount to as much as 40 % of the wage. In order to avoid paying this, the building trade, for example, employs Polish and Portugese workers on a temporary basis. They work for half the money, and the *Lohnnebenkosten* are saved.

20 I'll be back

The future

Ich werde bestimmt wiederkommen.
(= I'll definitely be back.)
It's very simple to talk about something that is going to happen in the future: werden + verb.

ich werde kommen
er / sie wird gehen
Sie werden essen
wir werden trinken

But there is a slight difficulty: werden is irregular.

Test your prejudices

What do you think of the Germans? Are they:

	a	b	
friendly			unfriendly
understanding			arrogant
naive			calculating
well dressed			badly dressed
generous			mean

Evaluation:

Five **a**s: You should pack your bags and move to Germany immediately. Five **b**s: Stay at home or go and settle in Papua New Guinea. Avoid Germany for the rest of your life. Two - four **a**s: Carry on as you are. Two - four **b**s: When are you going to change your life?

One of the first things that strikes visitors from abroad is the fact that Germany is a quiet country. Not of course on either side of the motorway. But in residential areas and in the pedestrian precincts of the town centres it is rarely very noisy, and people do in fact value their peace and quiet very highly; from ten o'clock in the evenings on no-one is supposed to keep their neighbours awake. If there is a party in a block of flats, this is often a source of conflict. In Bavaria it was debated for months whether the beer gardens should have to shut at ten or whether they should be allowed to stay open another couple of hours. Even the Prime Minister of Bavaria got involved – he supported the beer drinkers.

A common prejudice about Germans is that they are cold. But many visitors come away with quite the opposite impression.

Elsewhere in the world people talk about the Germans' hostility to foreigners. There is no doubt that this does exist, just as it does in England or France, and it's mainly targeted at foreigners in a weak position: refugees, asylum-seekers and those dependent on state support. However, Germans and non-Germans also live harmoniously alongside one another without any problem, the best example probably being the Kreuzberg district of Berlin, which is allegedly the largest Turkish town outside Turkey.

Some people are surprised how well organized Germany is. It is certainly true that the Germans like and are good at organizing, but this reputation is sometimes spoiled by Germans abroad who act as if they know better, fuelling the prejudice that the Germans are arrogant.

Let us hope that this is rarely experienced by visitors to Germany. There's nothing better for a country than a departing visitor who says, *Ich werde bestimmt wiederkommen* (= I'll definitely be back).

2/46

Deutschland ...Germany	gefallen .....to please
die Familie ....family	wiederkommen come back, come again
bestimmt .....definitely	am meisten ...most
die Weinstube ..wine bar	der Biergarten beer garden
der Alkoholiker alcoholic	es ist was los ...there's something
meinen ....to think, to mean	going on
lachen ....to laugh	auf Wiedersehen goodbye

Herr Muller? .... Mr Muller?

Hat es Ihnen in
Deutschland gefallen? .... Did you like Germany?

Ja, sehr. .... Yes, very much.

Warum fahren Sie
wieder nach Amerika? .... Why are you going back to
America?

Ich muss zu meiner Familie. .... I must go back to my family.

Werden Sie wiederkommen? ... Will you be coming back?

Sicher! Ich werde bestimmt
wiederkommen. .... Oh sure! I will
definitely come again.

Was hat Ihnen am meisten gefallen? What did you like most?

Die Weinstuben und die Biergärten. The wine bars and the beer gardens.

Sind Sie Alkoholiker? .... Are you an alcoholic?

Nein, aber da ist was los. .... No, but there's something
going on in them.

Wie meinen Sie das? .... What do you mean by that?

Die Leute trinken und
sprechen und lachen. .... People drink, talk and laugh.

Ja, die Deutschen
lachen nicht immer. .... Yes, the Germans don't always
laugh.

Das stimmt. .... That's true.

So, Sie müssen jetzt zum Bahnhof. .. Well, you must be off to
the station now.

Auf Wiedersehen. .... Goodbye.

Auf Wiedersehen,
bis zum nächsten Mal. .... Goodbye, till the next time.

gefallen (to please)

This verb, used to say that
you like something, is constructed like this:
Der Film gefällt mir. (singular)
Autos gefallen mir. (plural)

The past is as follows:
*Die Reise hat mir sehr gut
gefallen.*
*Diese Bücher haben mir
nicht gefallen.*

meinen (to think)

ich meine
er / sie meint
Sie meinen
wir meinen

lachen (to laugh)

ich lache
er / sie lacht
Sie lachen
wir lachen

The Germans also have the
saying *Lachen ist die beste
Medizin* (= Laughter is the
best medicine).
The opposite of *lachen* is
weinen (= to cry). It's conjugated just like *meinen*.

1. Put in the future tense

Ich werde **in den Biergarten gehen.**

1. in den Biergarten gehen
2. bestimmt wiederkommen
3. zum Bahnhof gehen
4. meine Familie wieder sehen
5. nach Zürich fahren
6. zum Arzt gehen
7. Kopfschmerzen haben
8. nicht mehr rauchen
9. nie mehr trinken
10. nicht sprechen

2. Find the right answer

1. Hat es Ihnen gefallen?
   a ■ Ja, sehr.
   b ■ Es gefällt mir nicht.

2. Werden Sie wiederkommen?
   a ■ Ja, bestimmt.
   b ■ Ja, ein bisschen.

3. Trinken Sie viel?
   a ■ Nein, ich trinke immer.
   b ■ Nein, ich trinke nie.

4. Lachen Sie viel?
   a ■ Lachen ist gesund.
   b ■ Die Deutschen lachen auch.

5. Haben Sie über Weinstuben gesprochen?
   a ■ Ja, wir haben über alles gesprochen.
   b ■ Nein, wir haben über Weinstuben gesprochen.

3. Complete the sentence

1. Die Leute
2. Sie müssen jetzt
3. Ich werde bestimmt
4. In den Biergärten
5. Warum kommen

a ■ Sie nicht wieder?
b ■ gerne wiederkommen.
c ■ lachen viel.
d ■ zum Bahnhof gehen.
e ■ ist was los.

4. A family makes plans

Wir werden **nach Österreich fahren.**

1. nach Österreich fahren
2. zusammen essen
3. den Freund vermissen
4. über alles reden
5. viel lachen
6. gut kochen und gut essen
7. im Supermarkt einkaufen
8. zusammen wegfahren

dich . . . . you
vermissen . . . . to miss
der Monat . . . . month
ohne . . . . without
lang . . . . long
vorher . . . . before
dir . . . . to you
schreiben . . . . to write
faxen . . . . to fax
Tschüs . . . . 'bye
mach's gut . . . . take care, all the best

Ich werde dich vermissen. . . . . . . I'll miss you.
Ich dich auch. . . . . I'll miss you, too.
Neun Monate ohne dich … . . . . Nine months without you …
Ja? . . . . Yes?
…das ist eine lange Zeit. . . . . …that's a long time.
Du arbeitest, ich arbeite. . . . . . . You're working, I'm working.
Ich weiß. . . . . I know.
Und ich habe eine Familie. . . . . . And I've got a family.
Ich weiß! . . . . I know!
Wir können uns
nicht vorher sehen. . . . . We won't be able
                                          to see each other before then.
Ich werde dir schreiben. . . . . I'll write to you.
Ich werde dich anrufen. . . . . I'll ring you.
Du kannst mir auch faxen. . . . . . You can also fax me.
Tschüs, ich muss jetzt gehen. . . . 'Bye, I must go now.
Tschüs. . . . . 'Bye.
Mach's gut. . . . . Take care.
Ich liebe dich… . . . . I love you…

du

Here it is at last, *du,* the 2nd person singular. It's used between friends, in the family, amongst young people and of course also between lovers.

du arbeitest, du schreibst, du bringst, du gehst, du verstehst, du kommst zurück

Irregular forms:
du fährst
du schläfst
du gibst (geben)
du siehst (sehen)

vermissen

This can be used for a person, but also for an object. *Ich vermisse meine Scheckkarte – muss ich jetzt zur Bank gehen?* (= I'm missing my bank card – do I have to go to the bank now?)

Preposition *ohne* + accusative
ich → ohne mich
Sie → ohne Sie
wir → ohne uns

new form:
du → dich

These two lovers have a bit of a problem: they live far apart and will not be able to see each other again in the near future. A bigger problem, however, is that he has a family. Well, that's men for you sometimes…

mach's gut – this is like *auf Wiedersehen* or *Tschüs,* another way of saying goodbye. It's only used colloquially, and only when people are on *du* terms with one another. People who say *Sie* to one another say *machen Sie's gut.* You only say this, however, when you know the other person really well.

1. *Das gefällt mir*

Der Film **gefällt mir** *gut.*

1. der Film / gut
2. das Buch / nicht
3. die Filmschauspieler / sehr
4. das Auto / besonders
5. die Zeitungen / nicht

Don't forget: when you like one thing then it's *gefällt*, when it's several things it must be *gefallen*. This of course also applies to people.

2. Translate into German

1. We'll miss you. _____
2. I can't see you before then. _____
3. I'll definitely be back. _____
4. People are talking and smoking. _____
5. You must be off to the station now. _____
6. Ten months is a long time. _____
7. Why don't you go to Germany? _____

Rather long sentences, but when you've learnt the vocabulary properly, studied the dialogues thoroughly and listened to them several times this translation shouldn't cause you any problems.

3. Put in the first person

Ich lache viel.

1. Wir lachen viel.
2. Sie werden wiederkommen.
3. Wir sprechen nicht.
4. Sie schreiben ein Buch.
5. Du kannst auch faxen.
6. Wir müssen jetzt gehen.
7. Sie lieben.

These sentences should be put in the first person.

4. You can say *du* to me

Du schreibst ein Buch.

1. Sie schreiben ein Buch.
2. Wir kommen morgen wieder.
3. Ich bringe das Geschenk.
4. Sie trinken Bier.
5. Wir arbeiten viel.
6. Sie lachen nie.

These sentences should be put in the *du*-form.

Völkerverständigung, international understanding, is a long word that describes a long drawn-out process. There must be an exchange between the people of the countries concerned, and the understanding must develop that leads to a collective friendship. At an individual level this is much simpler, always provided that people speak a common language – or can get by somehow.

It is said of the Germans that they do not make friends quickly. But those days are past, the world has drawn closer together, and for over 50 years there has been no war in Central Europe; between the younger generations of the various nations in particular there is no longer very much difference.

There is constant contact with other countries: business links, tourism, town twinning and contacts at club level are all ways in which people are brought together.

And while we're on the subject: the profoundest exchange is of course that between two people in love. Love certainly helps people learn a language and get to know another culture, and hence promotes understanding between nations. It is not unusual for a relationship to result in a mixed marriage, or in modern terms a bi-national partnership. This is not unproblematic. When a German woman marries an Arab, there are likely to be clashes of ideas about roles. But a mixed marriage is a unique opportunity: when the children grow up bilingual, when they perhaps commute between the countries concerned, this really does bring the nations of the world together.

Town-twinning arrangements are widespread in Europe: there are said to be over 5 000. The International Mayors Association that was founded in 1948 had a considerable influence on this development. It's obvious, local politicians also like the occasional jolly.

There's a society for people married to foreigners. It helps with serious problems, but not for example when the husband won't take the rubbish out.

Test 5

1. Which is right?

Look in a dictionary to find out what a *Linde* is.

1. *Lindenstraße* is
   a ■ a tree-lined avenue.
   b ■ a TV series.
   c ■ a novel.

You can actually get ZDF via satellite in many countries of the world.

2. ZDF, the *Zweites Deutsches Fernsehen,* is
   a ■ the largest broadcasting company in Europe.
   b ■ the best cultural channel in Germany.
   c ■ the most important commercial station.

This has to do with a new tendency in the way people live.

3. Today more and more people live
   a ■ at their workplace.
   b ■ in large families.
   c ■ alone and without a partner.

This is about new roles, which are actually old roles.

4. Married men
   a ■ almost never do the ironing.
   b ■ always take the rubbish out.
   c ■ don't earn any money of their own.

Of course this does not apply to everyone.

5. Foreigners in Germany suffer from
   a ■ wanderlust.
   b ■ circulatory problems.
   c ■ stomach problems.

What is the world coming to?

6. In Germany too
   a ■ the rich are becoming poorer.
   b ■ the poor are becoming richer.
   c ■ the rich are becoming richer.

2. Questions and answers

It's important that the answer makes sense. If you pick an answer that differs from the one suggested but had a particular idea in mind, that's all right too. Thinking should be rewarded.

1. Werden Sie wiederkommen?
2. Lieben Sie mich?
3. Wie geht es Ihrer Frau?
4. Haben Sie morgen Zeit?
5. Wo fehlt's denn?
6. Sind Sie krank?

a ■ Nein, ich liebe eine andere.
b ■ Ich habe Bauchschmerzen.
c ■ Nein, ich muss arbeiten.
d ■ Ich weiß nicht, wir leben getrennt.
e ■ Ja, nächstes Jahr bestimmt.
f ■ Ja, ich habe Bauchschmerzen.

3. Multiple choice

1. Der Bundeskanzler ist von einer Reise _____ .
   a ■ zurückkommen
   b ■ zurückgerufen
   c ■ zurückgekommen

Is the present or the past meant here?

2. Ich möchte Sie gerne _____ .
   a ■ einladen
   b ■ einmal
   c ■ eingeladen

Just because things sound similar, they don't have to mean the same thing. To say nothing of their grammatical function. The problem lies in the little ending.

3. Wie geht es _____ Frau?
   a ■ Ihren
   b ■ Ihrer
   c ■ Ihr

4. Sie müssen _____ zum Arzt.
   a ■ wo fehlt's
   b ■ nötig
   c ■ unbedingt

Only one solution fits.

5. Wir _____ gestern eingeladen.
   a ■ sind
   b ■ waren
   c ■ war

See number 2.

6. Wir _____ bestimmt wiederkommen.
   a ■ werden
   b ■ waren
   c ■ sind

Present, past or future?

4. Sense and nonsense

Some nonsense sounds like poetry. And some nonsense is certainly not devoid of meaning. It always depends on the context.

1. The wine bars and beer gardens are laughing.
2. The Federal Minister of Finance always has a headache.
3. The temperature and the hangover have separated.
4. I miss my backache.
5. The Pope and the Chancellor are smoking in the cinema.
6. I will definitely change my lawyer.

Key

1. Fill in the gaps 1. bitte – An important little word that is never out of place. 2. bin 3. bin – In the first person (*ich*) this is always the form the verb takes. 4. Sie – Here you are addressing a person you don't know and *sind* (= are) is the verb while *Sie* (= you) is the personal pronoun.

2. Find the right answer 1. b – *Aha* is what you say when you have just understood something. 2. b – *Nein, ich bin Herr Schroeder* would also be right. 3. b – *Entschuldigung* is not quite wrong, you can say that when you haven't quite understood something. 4. a – When someone wants to ask you something, then you reply *Ja, bitte?*, so the other solution *Guten Tag* doesn't fit here.

3. Sort into matching pairs 1. d 2. c 3. a 4. b

4. Make a sentence from these words 1. Ja, das bin ich. – *Ich bin das, ja* would also be possible. The *ja* can be put at the beginning or the end of the sentence. 2. Sind Sie Herr Seitz? – In a question the verb *sind* must always come at the beginning. 3. Ich bin Frau Krug. 4. Bin ich Thomas Schroeder? – This question is a bit odd, isn't it? As in English, in a question the verb comes first, then the person, then the rest.

5. What international words can you make? 1. com pu ter 2. ham bur ger 3. ra dio 4. te le fon 5. piz za 6. mu sik – This was a pretty easy exercise, wasn't it? Pity there are no prizes for getting it right!

1. Translate into English 1. Germany 2. America 3. Mexico 4. Japan 5. Italy 6. Israel 7. Syria 8. Australia 9. Austria – Have you noticed that most of the countries have similar names in English and German? Only *Deutschland* is completely different and *Österreich* has those funny dots over the o. *Reich* incidentally means empire.

2. Find the right answer 1. b – A reply to the question *woher?* (= where from?) must always contain a word for the direction: *aus* or *von* (= from). 2. a – It's a bit cheeky to answer a question with another one. 3. b – In reply to the question asking you your name it sounds silly to answer with the country you come from. If you don't understand, it's better to say *Entschuldigung?* 4. b – Did you know that Hamburg is not in Italy but in Germany?

3. Sort into matching pairs 1. c 2. d 3. e 4. a 5. b – If you've made more than one mistake here, then you should study the vocabulary again.

4. What's your name? 1. Ich heiße Hans Schröder. 2. Ich heiße Detlef Barber. 3. Ich heiße Steffi Graf. – the most famous woman tennis-player 4. Ich heiße Helmut Kohl. – Conservative Federal Chancellor since 1982 5. Ich heiße Michael Schumacher. – Formula I driver 6. Ich heiße Johann Wolfgang von Goethe. – poet and playwright (1749–1832) 7. Ich heiße Nina Hagen. – rock singer always getting involved in some scandal or other 8. Ich heiße Egon Krause. – friend of the author 9. Ich heiße Wolfgang Amadeus Mozart. – composer 1756–1791

5. Where are you from? 1. Ich komme aus Amerika. 2. Ich komme aus Deutschland. 3. Ich komme aus Australien. 4. Ich komme aus Italien. 5. Ich komme aus Israel. 6. Ich komme aus Österreich. 7. Ich komme aus Mexiko. 8. Ich komme aus Japan. 9. Ich komme aus Syrien.

1. Fill in the gaps 1. kommen – You can also ask *Woher sind Sie?*, it means the same thing. 2. Name – On forms you will find *Vornamen und Nachnamen* (= Christian name and surname) 3. geht – The literal translation of this is "How goes it you?" 4. schön – unfortunately not always and not for everyone.

2. Find the right answer 1. a – Answer b makes no sense at all 2. b – If someone is asked if her name is Schumacher she can hardly answer *Alles in Ordnung, Frau Schumacher.* Instead of *Ja, das bin ich* you could also say *Ja, ich bin das.* 3. a – You can't answer a question with another one, not at least unless you don't want to answer. 4. b – The answer *Ja, ich heiße…* would not be wrong if it didn't end with another name.

3. Sort into matching pairs 1. c 2. a 3. d 4. b

4. How are you? 1. Danke, gut. 2. Danke, nicht so gut. 3. Danke, sehr gut. 4. Danke, wunderbar. 5. Danke, alles in Ordnung.

1. Sort into matching pairs – If you are not sure, then it's better to look at the vocabulary again. You will also find a dictionary in the appendix with all the words in alphabetical order. 1. e 2. d 3. c 4. b 5. a

2. Find the right answer 1. b – *Danke aus Deutschland* is pretty illogical. 2. b – *Ja, wunderbar* would only be appropriate if someone had been saved from something unpleasant by the illness, such as an exam, a tiresome piece of work or an unpleasant meeting … 3. a – *Kein Problem* is perhaps rather a short answer, but it fits here. You can hardly answer a question about how you are with a remark connected with your name, so b has to be wrong. 4. b – *Hallo* can be said at any time of the day or night, but only as a greeting. *Guten Morgen* can also be used when you are saying goodbye.

3. Translate into English 1. wonderful 2. not so good 3. it's not a problem / no problem 4. life 5. really 6. maybe a bit 7. everything okay? 8. great

4. How are you? 1. Danke, es geht gut. 2. Danke, es geht wunderbar. 3. Danke, es geht sehr gut. 4. Danke, es geht nicht so gut.

5. Ask questions 1. Sind Sie aus Amerika? 2. Sind Sie krank? 3. Sind Sie Herr Schroeder? 4. Sind Sie aus Italien? 5. Sind Sie Frau Krause? 6. Sind Sie nicht krank?

1. Sort into pairs 1. d 2. c 3. b 4. a – Not difficult, is it?

2. Give the English translation 1. very nice 2. newspaper 3. computer 4. I don't understand. 5. What do you do? 6. I work 7. Excuse me 8. Where are you from?

3. The right answer 1. b – Answer a is also conceivable and not absolutely wrong. 2. a – Your occupation has nothing to do with where you're from. 3. b – Your occupation also has nothing to do with your name. 4. a – The question for answer b would be: *Kommen Sie?* (= Are you coming?)

4. You → I 1. ich mache 2. ich arbeite 3. ich bin. – *Sein* (= to be) is the only completely irregular verb. The first person does not end in -e and the third does not end in -en 4. ich verstehe 5. ich komme 6. ich weiß

1. Sort into pairs 1. e 2. f 3. c 4. a 5. d 6. b

2. What are you? 1. Ich bin Fotograf. 2. Ich bin Journalist. 3. Ich bin Student. 4. Ich bin Ingenieur. 5. Ich bin Amerikaner. – If this sort of exercise seems a bit silly to you, then say it out loud, since it will help you get used to the German pronunciation.

3. Find the right answer 1. a – *Ich arbeite* hasn't got much to do with the question, but someone might say it who doesn't want to be disturbed, as in *Lass mich bitte in Ruhe, ich arbeite* (= Please leave me alone, I'm working). 2. a – *Ja, das bin ich* answers the question *Sind Sie Herr oder Frau X?* 3. b – The statement that you aren't working also answers the question about your occupation. Also possible would be *Ja, das bin ich* or *Nein, das bin ich nicht.* 4. b – This is not a proper answer, but a way out when you don't want to give one.

4. What about the women? 1. Journalistin 2. Studentin 3. Fotografin 4. Ingenieurin – Today you must pay attention to the gender of the person you are talking about. *Frau Hinz ist Fotograf*

doesn't sound right, you must of course say *Frau Hinz ist Fotografin*. The language has changed and older people who can remember a time when fewer women went to work sometimes leave the *-in* off. They're in real trouble if a feminist hears them!

5. I → you 1. Sie heißen 2. Sie kommen 3. Sie arbeiten 4. Sie verstehen 5. Sie machen 6. Sie sind

4   Exercises A

1. Translate into German 1. neugierig 2. verheiratet 3. Frage 4. Ingenieur 5. wirklich 6. aber 7. schlimm 8. krank

2. Do you have a …? 1. Haben Sie eine Frage? 2. Haben Sie eine Zeitung? 3. Haben Sie eine Frau? 4. Haben Sie eine Pizza? 5. Haben Sie eine Bank? 6. Haben Sie eine Information? – For all feminine nouns *die,* as already mentioned, is the definite article, *eine* the indefinite article. *Die Frau im Café* (= the woman in the café) is a particular woman, *Ich sehe eine Frau* (= I see a woman) is any woman, one who has not been specified in any way.

3. Sort into matching pairs 1. c – Have you noticed that, as in English, questions that are whole sentences containing a verb and a person are always answered with *ja* or *nein,* while questions consisting of single words *wo, wie, woher, was* (= where, how, where from, what) etc. are always answered with a statement. 2. d – This dialogue is admittedly a bit odd. *Sind Sie verheiratet? Ja, mein Mann ist aber in Berlin.* There is evidently some flirting going on here. 3. e – The answer that you are not working is also a suitable reply when you are asked about your occupation. 4. b – Some spell it with *ö* and *s* at the end, others with *ü.* 5. a – It's logical that when you're ill everything's not okay.

4. That's not my … 1. Das ist nicht mein Problem. 2. Das ist nicht mein Mann. 3. Das ist nicht mein Leben. 4. Das ist nicht mein Computer. 5. Das ist nicht mein Foto. 6. Das ist nicht mein Radio.

4   Exercises B

1. Which answer is right? 1. b – If a man has a wife, he normally lives with her. There are of course also cases where a man and woman are married but live apart. Perhaps because they get on better that way, or because they are not yet divorced, or because one works where the other one does not want to live. 2. a – A photographer works mainly with a camera and in the darkroom. Admittedly today there are also photographers who work with a computer. 3. a – Do not confuse *Frau* and *Frage*. 4. a – *Krank* and *neugierig* have little to do with one another, unless someone is pathologically curious. Then only therapy can help. Although there's a saying in German that curiosity is the mother of science.

2. A little German translation 1. Ich arbeite alleine. – It's not a literal translation we're looking for here, but the correct and idiomatic way of saying something. 2. Herr Schulz ist neugierig. 3. Fred ist krank. 4. Ich habe ein Problem. 5. Das ist wunderbar.

3. What's missing? 1. Freundin 2. Problem 3. Frage 4. Zeitung 5. Stress

4. Which is the odd one out? 1. Leben – The other words all refer to people. 2. Freundin – The others are all occupations and men, although being a student is admittedly not always an occupation. 3. schlimm – Because it really isn't a positive word 4. bisschen – It ends in *-en,* but it isn't a verb. 5. Zeitung – This doesn't fit here, because it isn't an international word. If you picked *Musik* you would also be right, as all the other words refer to modern communication media. Now the clever ones are going to say: *Aber Musik ist doch auch ein modernes Kommunikationsmedium!* (= But music is also a modern communication medium!) And the clever ones are of course right, too. 20 points for the winners.

T   Test 1

1. Which is right? 1. c 2. a 3. b 4. c 5. c 6. b

2. Answer and question 1. c 2. d 3. a 4. b 5. f 6. e

3. Multiple choice 1. b 2. b 3. a 4. c 5. a 6. c

4. Sense and nonsense 1. Mein Name ist Student. 2. Ich habe eine Entschuldigung. 3. Ist alles interessant in Berlin? 4. Das Leben ist so krank! 5. Kein Problem, Frau Zeitung. 6. Ich verstehe vielleicht.

1. Sort into pairs 1. c – Note that the number *sechs* (6) is pronounced exactly like "sex" (same word in German). This is of course a source of endless jokes. 2. d – *acht* and *Achtung,* which means "watch out!", have the same pronunciation. 3. e – Not to be confused with *nein* (= no). 4. f 5. g 6. h 7. a – *fünf* (5) is the number that is hardest to pronounce correctly: not everyone can immediately say the *ü* with its umlaut, and what is actually said is *füm-pf.* 8. b.

2. Fill in 1. Zwei und drei ist fünf. 2. Eins und sieben ist acht. 3. Vier und zwei ist sechs. 4. Fünf und zwei ist sieben. 5. Drei und sechs ist neun. – If you get the sums wrong there's not much we can do, except suggest you repeat the second year of primary school.

3. What do you need? 1. Ich brauche ein Telefon. 2. Ich brauche eine Zeitung. 3. Ich brauche einen Computer. – Actually it's *ein Computer,* but brauchen takes the accusative, so it's *einen.* 4. Ich brauche ein Foto. 5. Ich brauche eine Freundin. – We hope this is a sentence you won't ever have to use, and the same goes for *Ich brauche einen Freund.* 6. Ich brauche Ihren Namen. 7. Ich brauche Ihre Telefonnummer. 8. Ich brauche die Vorwahl von Berlin.

4. Can I ...? 1. Kann ich telefonieren? – Normally what you would say is *Kann ich mal* (= *einmal* = once) *telefonieren?* See comment in the margin for Lesson 3, dialogue B. 2. Kann ich am Computer arbeiten? 3. Kann ich eine Zeitung haben? – When the author is sitting in a café this is what he sometimes says to the waiter. 4. Kann ich morgen kommen? 5. Kann ich das verstehen? 6. Kann ich in Hamburg leben? 7. Kann ich mal raten? – Look back to the first sentence. 8. Kann ich Ihre Telefonnummer haben? – Not necessarily a question to be asked after the first couple of minutes.

5. What is the next number? 1. acht 2. sechs 3. zwei 4. zehn 5. fünf 6. vier 7. sieben – Whenever you have a spare moment, when you are sitting in the underground looking out of the window, when the ads come on during a film on TV, or while you are blocking your ears to one of your boss's tirades, use the time to practise the numbers forwards and backwards, at least in your mind.

1. Find the translation 1. c 2. e 3. b 4. a 5. d – There's no harm in imagining the situation that might go with each command. For example: 1. answering machine, 2. on the phone, or when you're in your boss's office, 3. what a slacker might be told, 4. what someone says who wants to make a bit of news exciting, 5. could be an invitation, or perhaps an enticement.

2. Which is the right answer? 1. a – b would also be possible if the sentence was *Nein, ich bin um acht hier.* 2. b – *Ja, sie ist hier* would also be possible. 3. b – The code and the telephone number are not the same thing. The situation here is as follows: the two people who are talking are both in Frankfurt. 4. b – If the sentence had been *Ich habe kein Telefon,* then a) would also have been possible.

3. Give the German for it 1. um acht Uhr 2. das Zimmer 3. zurückrufen 4. er 5. natürlich 6. morgen 7. die Vorwahl. – For this exercise you just have to swot up on vocabulary.

4. Read the telephone number in German 1. drei-zwei-eins-sechs-acht-neun 2. sieben-neun-zwei-eins-fünf-vier 3. sechs-acht-zwei-vier-eins-sechs 4. neun-zwei-eins-acht-fünf-sechs 5. neun-acht-zwei-fünf-sieben-drei 6. sieben-fünf-drei-eins-neun-sieben 7. zwei-vier-sechs-acht-zwei-vier 8. eins-zwei-neun-acht-sechs-fünf. – In big cities the telephone number is longer. Within Germany a number might be as long as 0611-2344567.

5. Ask questions 1. Können Sie morgen anrufen? – That's what someone might be told who is ringing at the wrong time. **2. Können Sie gut Deutsch sprechen?** – That's what a non-native speaker would ask. The native speaker soon notices if someone can speak well or not. **3. Können Sie um neun kommen?** – A suggestion for a meeting. **4. Können Sie die Arbeit machen?** – An attempt to persuade someone, or a friendly way of giving a command. When the other person can't say *nein,* then he has to do the work. **5. Können Sie das verstehen?** – This question might be arrogant or it might just be a friendly offer to repeat what's just been said and explain it. .

6 Exercises A

1. Can I get … here? 1. Kann ich hier Zeitungen bekommen? 2. Kann ich hier Briefmarken bekommen? 3. Kann ich hier Postkarten bekommen? 4. Kann ich hier Telefonkarten bekommen? 5. Kann ich hier Hamburger bekommen? 6. Kann ich hier Computer bekommen? 7. Kann ich hier Telefone bekommen? 8. Kann ich hier Radios bekommen? – These questions are what you ask when you are actually in the shop. On the telephone you would ask, *Kann ich bei Ihnen* (= at your shop/establishment) *… bekommen?* 9. Kann ich hier Probleme bekommen? – This is what you would say, for example, when you're parking your car somewhere where it's not allowed, and you're checking with someone whether the police would normally tow it away. It would also be appropriate in many other situations.

2. Find the right answer The questions all begin with *haben,* in other words with a verb. They are complete sentences, so the answer must always include or imply *ja* or *nein.* **1.** a **2.** a – What is actually meant is *Nein, ich habe nur Briefmarken.* **3.** b – Here *natürlich* is a way of saying *ja* with particular emphasis. **4.** b

3. Sort into matching pairs 1. c 2. e 3. d 4. a 5. b – You won't have any problem finding what goes together. Try and do this exercise without mentally translating every word.

4. How much is it? 1. Neun Zeitungen, das macht achtzehn Mark. 2. Zwei Pizzas, das macht sechzehn Mark. 3. Zehn Briefmarken, das macht zwanzig Mark. 4. Drei Postkarten, das macht neun Mark. 5. Drei Fragen, das macht null Mark. 6. Eine Zeitung, das macht zwei Mark. 7. Eine Pizza, das macht acht Mark. 8. Eine Briefmarke, das macht zwei Mark. 9. Eine Postkarte, das macht drei Mark. 10. Eine Frage, das macht null Mark. – If you have more than one mistake with questions 6-10, the same advice applies as for exercise 2 in Unit 5 A.

6 Exercises B

1. Find the right answer Answer c could of course be given to every question. So distribute all the other answers first and use it for the question that is left over. **1.** d **2.** c – Only this answer fits here. **3.** a **4.** e **5.** b. – The question *wo?* can of course only be answered with a place.

2. Give some advice 1. Am besten Sie nehmen ein Taxi. 2. Am besten Sie nehmen eine Zeitung. 3. Am besten Sie nehmen einen Computer. 4. Am besten Sie nehmen ein Hotel. 5. Am besten Sie nehmen eine Briefmarke. 6. Am besten Sie nehmen einen Hamburger. 7. Am besten Sie nehmen ein Zimmer. 8. Am besten Sie nehmen eine Freundin. 9. Am besten Sie nehmen einen Student. – 8. and 9. could be answers to a question such as *Ich brauche einen Babysitter.*

3. Take away 1. Achtzehn minus zwölf ist sechs. 2. Neunzehn minus vierzehn ist fünf. 3. Zwölf minus elf ist eins. 4. Zwanzig minus siebzehn ist drei. 5. Sechzehn minus dreizehn ist drei. 6. Fünfzehn minus Fünfzehn ist null. – Instead of minus you can also say *weniger* (= less): *Drei weniger zwei ist eins.*

4. Apologize 1. Tut mir Leid, ich habe kein Telefon. – There are still people who have no telephone. 2. Tut mir Leid, ich habe keine Telefonkarte. – That's your own fault; you should always have a phone card with you. With fewer and fewer coin-operated public telephones, you don't really have any choice in the matter. 3. Tut mir Leid, ich habe keine Zeitung. – This is what the waiter says in reply to sentence 3 of exercise 4 in Unit 5 A. **4. Tut mir Leid, ich habe keine Briefmarke.** – That would be embarrassing if it came from the post office clerk. **5. Tut mir Leid, ich habe kein Buch.** – An intellectual's little joke. **6. Tut mir Leid, ich habe kein Fax.** – It doesn't matter, it happens in the best circles. **7. Tut mir Leid, ich habe keinen Brief.**

5. Fill in the gaps **1. Tut mir Leid, ich habe keine Bücher.** – Singular *kein Buch,* plural *keine Bücher.* **2. Vier und fünf, das macht neun Mark.** – Full marks for your arithmetic! **3. Am besten Sie nehmen ein Taxi.** – You can say either *mit dem Taxi fahren* or *ein Taxi nehmen.* **4. Wo bekomme ich Briefmarken?** – *Wo kann ich Briefmarken kaufen?* would also be possible **5. Kann ich ein Fax senden?** – *Der Sender,* by the way, is a radio or TV station.

1. What's the missing number? 1. vierzig 2. sechzig 3. siebzig 4. neunzig. – In order to practise counting the tens, see the recommendation in the 5th exercise in Unit 5A.

2. Find the right answer If you learn your numbers thoroughly, no-one will be able to cheat you. Here you've got to check the sums. 1. b 2. b 3. a 4. b

3. Answer with "yes" 1. Ja, ich brauche ein Brot. 2. Ja, ich heiße Mayer. 3. Ja, ich komme morgen. 4. Ja, ich bin Fotografin. 5. Ja, ich spreche ein bisschen Deutsch. 6. Ja, ich wünsche Butter. 7. Ja, ich rufe zurück. 8. Ja, ich nehme Weißbrot. 9. Ja, ich sende ein Fax. 10. For the next part you must establish whether it's a noun (with an *ein* that becomes *kein*) or a verb (adding a *nicht*) you are putting in the negative form: 1. Nein, ich brauche kein Brot. 2. Nein, ich heiße nicht Mayer. 3. Nein, ich komme morgen nicht. 4. Nein, ich bin keine Fotografin. 5. Nein, ich spreche kein bisschen Deutsch. – The opposite of *ein bisschen* is *kein bisschen.* 6. Nein, ich wünsche keine Butter. 7. Nein, ich rufe nicht zurück. 8. Nein, ich nehme kein Weißbrot. 9. Nein, ich sende kein Fax.

4. Say what you prefer These sentences are shortened statements such as *Nein, ich wünsche kein …, lieber ein … .* In other words the noun must be in the accusative with the *ein* taking the ending *-en* if it's a masculine noun. 1. Nein, kein Weißbrot, lieber ein Vollkornbrot. 2. Nein, kein Brot, lieber einen Käse. 3. Nein, keine Zeitung, lieber ein Buch. 4. Nein, keine Postkarte, lieber einen Brief. 5. Nein, keinen Brief, lieber ein Fax.

1. What's missing? 1. Vollkornbrot 2. Rotwein 3. Problem 4. zurückrufen – There are other verbs with the prefix *zurück,* such as *zurücksenden, zurücknehmen, zurückbekommen* (= send back, take back, get back). 5. Buchhandlung 6. die Telefonkarte 7. das Weißbrot 8. interessant

2. Which answer is right? 1. b. – This is short for *Nein, ich brauche kein Brot, ich brauche Rotwein.* 2. b – The sales assistant is asking you if it can be a bit over, so you don't need to repeat this. It would also be correct to say, *Ja, lieber mehr* (= Yes, I'd rather have more). 3. a – The person who asks *Sonst noch was?* is the one doing the selling, so the customer answers *Ich brauche …* 4. b – Grammatically a is also possible, but a negative answer like this would hardly be polite.

3. Find the partners 1. e 2. c 3. g 4. f 5. a 6. b 7. d – In the opinion of the author, incidentally, cheese goes just as well with white bread as with red wine. It's all a matter of taste.

4. What else do you need? This is how you tell the sales assistant that it is not three kilos of cheese or 15 bottles of wine or five loaves you need but only *ein bisschen* of each. 1. Ich brauche noch ein bisschen Käse. 2. Ich brauche noch ein bisschen Brot. 3. Ich brauche noch ein bisschen Wurst. 4. Ich brauche noch ein bisschen Butter. 5. Ich brauche noch ein bisschen Wein. 6. Ich brauche noch ein bisschen Salami.

5. Ask politely for … 1. Geben Sie mir bitte etwas Brot. 2. Geben Sie mir bitte etwas Wurst. 3. Geben Sie mir bitte etwas Butter. 4. Geben Sie mir bitte etwas Salami. 5. Geben

Sie mir bitte etwas Käse. 6. Geben Sie mir bitte etwas Wein. – In all these sentences you could also say *ein bisschen* instead of *etwas*.

1. Suggestions beginning with Let's go … If someone doesn't know what to do and says "what shall we do now", it is always appropriate to make a suggestion starting with *Gehen wir…* 1. Gehen wir einkaufen. 2. Gehen wir ein Fax senden. 3. Gehen wir arbeiten. 4. Gehen wir Geld wechseln. 5. Gehen wir mit Maria sprechen. 6. Gehen wir alles zahlen. – Assuming you're not one of those who don't pay their bills! 7. Gehen wir Peter anrufen.

2. Say no: *kein* or *kein-e?* 1. Ich habe kein Geld 2. Ich habe keine Butter. 3. Ich bin kein Journalist. 4. Ich habe kein Problem. 5. Ich kaufe kein Geschenk. 6. Ich brauche kein Geld. 7. Ich höre kein Radio. – With *haben, kein* is in the accusative, with *sein* in the nominative. This only makes a difference with masculine nouns in the singular, as in *Haben Sie keinen Freund? Ich bin kein Freund.*

3. Translate into German 1. Tut mir Leid, ich habe kein Geld. 2. Gehen wir Geld wechseln. 3. Ich brauche Briefmarken. 4. Ich kaufe Käse und Schinken. 5. Geben Sie mir Rotwein. 6. Sie sind neugierig. 7. Ich zahle mit der Kreditkarte. – If you have written *mit Kreditkarte* this is also right. The *der* is actually the dative of *die,* which must always be used after *mit;* this will all sound very complicated for the moment.

4. What have you forgotten? 1. Ich habe die Zeitung vergessen. 2. Ich habe das Geschenk vergessen. – That's something you shouldn't do when you're invited somewhere. 3. Ich habe den Student vergessen. 4. Ich habe das Buch vergessen. – That's something you shouldn't do when you've borrowed a book. 5. Ich habe die Frage vergessen. 6. Ich habe meine Frau vergessen. – That's something you shouldn't do if you want to grow old with her.

5. What is the missing verb? It's always useful to picture the situation concerned, for example, in the first sentence you might be a smoker and need a box of matches which costs 20 pfennigs, but you haven't got any German money. 1. zahlen 2. wechseln 3. kaufen 4. senden.

1. Find the right answer 1. b – Sentence a does have something to do with money, but nothing to do with the question about the exchange rate. And the person asking it is the one who wants to change money. 2. b – The commission is sometimes a real problem when you only need 50 marks, and then pay almost half of it in commission when you change your pounds or dollars. 3. a – b is not totally wrong, as the person changing money is in practice selling. But it would be better to say, *Ja, wir verkaufen Dollars.* 4. a. – b is not quite wrong either, but the sentence would have to be *Ja, ich brauche das Geld jetzt, nicht morgen.*

2. Sort into matching pairs 1. d 2. c 3. a 4. b. – Be thankful that you haven't got to write numbers like 123,456 yet: *einhundertdreiundzwanzigtausendvierhundertsechsundfünfzig.*

3. Say what you want 1. Ich möchte ein Buch kaufen. 2. Ich möchte das verstehen. 3. Ich möchte Michael Jackson heißen. – When you say this sentence, you haven't got to agree with it, it's just a grammar exercise. 4. Ich möchte Ingenieur sein. 5. Ich möchte ein Geschenk bekommen. – Who wouldn't? 6. Ich möchte 200 Dollars wechseln. 7. Ich möchte morgen alleine kommen. – What could be behind that? 8. Ich möchte am Computer arbeiten. – That's what the author is doing, but he would rather go for a walk in the woods than always be sitting in front of the monitor. 9. Ich möchte mit Kreditkarte zahlen. 10. Ich möchte einkaufen gehen.

4. Write out and read these numbers 1. zwölf 2. dreiundzwanzig 3. vierunddreißig 4. fünfundvierzig 5. sechsundfünfzig 6. siebenundsechzig 7. achtundsiebzig 8. neunundachtzig. – We hope you've now more or less mastered the numbers up to 100.

1. Which is right? 1. b 2. b 3. c 4. b 5. a 6. c
2. Answers and questions 1. f 2. e 3. d 4. c 5. b 6. a
3. Multiple choice 1. c 2. c 3. b 4. a 5. b 6. a
4. Sense and nonsense 1. Ich möchte ein Vollkornbrot mit Entschuldigung. 2. Brauchen Sie 200 Gramm Reiseschecks? 3. Gehen wir Kreditkarten leben. 4. Nehmen Sie Weißbrot oder Computer? 5. Das Problem ist wunderbar. 6. Sprechen Sie Rotwein?

A Exercises   9

1. Translate into German 1. geradeaus 2. sehr schwierig 3. der Bahnhof – When you are out and about, make a short list of buildings to give yourself a repertoire for travelling purposes. 4. zweite Straße links – When you know *rechts, links* and *geradeaus,* you will theoretically always be able to find your way around. Theoretically. Other important words are *an der Ampel* (= at the traffic lights) and *an der Kreuzung* (= at the junction). 5. Fragen Sie wieder! – *Wieder* expresses repetition: *Kommen Sie wieder. Noch einmal* is also possible: *Fragen Sie noch einmal! – Ich habe Sie nicht verstanden* (= Ask again! – I didn't understand you).
2. Which question is right? 1. a – This is a bit mean: the answer is not about stamps, but about books. So the second question does not fit. 2. a – If the answer had been *Nur 50 Mark,* the second question would have been right. 3. a – The question *Wie viele?* cannot be answered with an ordinal number (first, second, third …), but only with a cardinal number (one, two, a thousand …). *Die zweite/dritte/vierte Straße links* or *rechts* is what you would say in response to a request for directions. 4. b – The answer is a time, so the question about the telephone cannot be right.
3. Ordinal numbers 1. Helmut Kohl ist der sechste Bundeskanzler von Deutschland. – Since 1996 he has incidentally been in office longer than the first Federal Chancellor, Konrad Adenauer. 2. Meine zweite Frau heißt Maria. – If someone says this, he's either divorced or married to several women. 3. Ich habe noch eine dritte Frage. – Someone who asks questions is curious, and someone who asks three times really is interested. 4. Papst Johannes der dreiundzwanzigste. (XXIII.) – Not everyone knows the Roman numbers: I, II, III, IV, V, VI … although they are used as ordinal numbers in all European countries.
4. Find the opposites 1. h 2. g 3. f 4. e 5. d 6. c 7. b 8. a 9. j. – Normally it would be *schlecht,* another word for bad, but you haven't learnt this word yet so we'll allow *schlimm* here. 10. i.

B Exercises   9

1. How does the sentence continue? 1. b – c would also be a possible answer, so would a and d if they were not followed by a question mark. 2. c 3. a – Grammatically d would also be possible, but this does not make much sense unless you are using *Fax* in the sense of fax machine. 4. e – c would also be possible. 5 d – a would also be possible, but better with something added such as *nach Amerika gesendet?* or *an Herrn Dupont gesendet?*
2. Which answer is right? Remember that if a normal sentence, in other words a sentence that is not a question, does not begin with the subject, i.e. the person or thing that's doing something, then the verb is always in second place. This does not of course mean it's always the second word: *In Ihrem Hotel wohnen auch zwei Franzosen* (= There are also two Frenchmen staying at your hotel). Here for example the verb *wohnen* is in the second place but as the fourth word. 1. a 2. b 3. b 4. b 5. b
3. Fill in the gaps 1. Idee 2. Reisebüro 3. nach – This is something the English and Americans often get wrong, saying *zu* instead of *nach.* When we are talking about towns, countries etc. it must always be *nach: Fahren Sie nach Berlin? Zu* is used for persons: *Ich fahre zu meinem Onkel* (= I'm going to my uncle's). 4. dritte 5. Urlaub – There is another word for this, *die Ferien: Jetzt können Sie keine Ferien machen* (= You can't go on holiday now). *Ferien* is always in the plural. 6. schwierig – A lot of

things can be *schwierig, die Frage, das Problem, die Arbeit,* and of course also *ein Mensch* (= a person).

4. Put in the past tense All six are so-called weak verbs, which form the past participle with *ge-* and *-t.*
1. Ich habe ein Buch gekauft. 2. Ich habe das nicht geglaubt. 3. Ich habe in Berlin gelebt. 4. Ich habe zwanzig D-Mark gewechselt. 5. Ich habe mit der Kreditkarte gezahlt. 6. Ich habe Urlaub gemacht. – Can you still remember the second word for holiday? If not, look at the solutions to the last exercise.

1. When does the train leave? – For the time being you actually only need the numbers 1 to 59, but it doesn't hurt to know the others, in order for example to say the date. 1. Um sechs Uhr fünfzehn. 2. Um vierzehn Uhr dreiundzwanzig. 3. Um null Uhr vierundvierzig. 4. Um sieben Uhr dreißig. 5. Um zehn Uhr sechzehn. 6. Um einundzwanzig Uhr zweiundzwanzig. 7. Um fünf Uhr dreiundvierzig. 8. Um neunzehn Uhr neunundfünfzig. 9. Um zwölf Uhr zehn.

2. Find the right answer 1. b – With *Wohin* you ask about a place away from you. The answer cannot therefore be: *Ich komme aus,* i.e. from another place to here. 2. b – a would have been right if it had been *Ja, ich habe nämlich noch keine* (= Yes, I haven't got one yet). 3. a – b would have been right if it had been: *Nein, wir fahren mit dem Auto.* 4. a – Whether you now have a ticket or not has nothing to do with the question about the time. b must therefore be wrong.

3. Ask questions Envisage the situations suggested in brackets. 1. Ist der Zug voll? (At the ticket office window) 2. Ist die Idee gut? (During a discussion at work or after seven beers) 3. Ist der Journalist neugierig? (The editor of the newspaper wants to know this before he employs the journalist.) 4. Ist der Doktor krank? (20 people have already been waiting over four hours in the surgery waiting room). 5. Ist das Zimmer schön? (The person you are speaking to already knows the hotel you want to go to.) 6. Ist der Student verheiratet? (You often see him with a woman and a pram.) 7. Ist der Dollarkurs interessant? (Perhaps you would like to change 3000 dollars and if the rate is going up, then it might be worthwhile.) 8. Ist das Problem schwierig? (You are checking in half an hour before the plane leaves and have just noticed that you've left your passport at home.)

4. Find the partners There is only one possibility for completing number 5, but two alternatives for all the others. 1. d (e) 2. a (c) 3. e (d) – There are people who love pondering over problems. c is not possible, as it would then have to be ein-e gute Idee. 4. c (a) 5. b

1. Put in the correct order It is of course easy when a *der* or *die* or a verb starts with a capital letter, or when *Klasse* is followed by ? Then you at least know what the first or last word is. 1. Die Maschine geht in fünfzehn Minuten. 2. Fahren Sie zweiter Klasse? 3. Der Zug ist nicht sehr voll. 4. Möchten Sie eine Reservierung? 5. Kann ich hier einchecken?

2. What is it in English? 1. the luggage 2. that depends 3. the plane 4. the exit 5. the ticket 6. damn 7. which 8. to travel, go (by train/car/plane) 9. the train 10. full

3. At what time? If you're in a bus or standing in a lift, look at your watch from time to time and tell yourself the time correctly in German. 1. Um vier Uhr fünfunddreißig. 2. Um fünfzehn Uhr sechsundvierzig. 3. Um dreiundzwanzig Uhr siebenundfünfzig. 4. Um ein Uhr sechzehn. 5. Um neun Uhr dreiunddreißig. 6. Um dreizehn Uhr fünf. 7. Um siebzehn Uhr achtzehn. 8. Um neunzehn Uhr fünfundvierzig.

4. Put in the past tense 1. Sie haben Rotwein gekauft. 2. Sie haben die Frage vergessen. – *Vergessen* is a strong verb, and the past participle doesn't end in *-t* but *-en.* 3. Sie haben sehr viel gearbeitet. 4. Sie haben in Frankreich gelebt. 5. Sie haben nicht gehört. 6. Sie haben Geld gebraucht.

5. What's missing? Of course other solutions are possible here too. But you should only complete the exercise with words you know. 1. einchecken – Here of course any verb would fit. 2. Klasse 3. Maschine. 4. Der Zug – *ICE* would also be possible 5. Minuten or Stunden.

1. Doing something for the first time The verb must always be in the first person. With *sein* this is irregular, and with *anrufen,* a separable verb, the prefix *an* goes to the end of the sentence. 1. Ich bin zum ersten Mal in Osnabrück. 2. Ich fahre zum ersten Mal mit dem ICE. 3. Ich arbeite zum ersten Mal am Computer. 4. Ich sende zum ersten Mal ein Fax. 5. Ich verstehe das zum ersten Mal. 6. Ich kaufe zum ersten Mal ein Flugzeug. 7. Ich zahle zum ersten Mal mit Kreditkarte. 8. Ich komme zum ersten Mal nach Berlin. 9. Ich rufe zum ersten Mal Maria an.
2. Which answer is right? 1. b – You're sitting in a taxi and say *Ich fahre mit dem Bus.* This is either meaningless or surreal. The question about the currency indicates that the passenger is a foreigner. 2. a – *Manchmal* may sound similar, but it has nothing to do with *zum ersten Mal.* 3. a – b would make sense if it was *Ich spreche nur Deutsch.* 4. b – a would only be possible in answer to the question *Fahren Sie mit dem Taxi?* or *Nehmen Sie ein Taxi?.*
3. Where is it? 1. Hier ist das Telefon. 2. Rechts ist das Hotel. 3. Dort drüben ist der Ausgang. – *Hier* is always near the speaker, *dort* at some distance from the speaker. 4. Links ist der Bahnhof. 5. Rechts ist die Bank. 6. Hier ist das Reisebüro. 7. Dort ist das Gepäck. 8. Links ist der Computer.
4. *(k)ein, (k)eine* or *(k)einen?* 1. ein 2. eine 3. ein 4. keine 5. eine 6. kein, einen 7. ein 8. keine 9. kein 10. einen. – Have patience, it takes a while until these little endings come automatically. When you hear someone speaking German, ask yourself from time to time, why is he saying *kein,* why *kein-e* why *kein-en*? Ah, of course, it's *der Computer,* ah, *die Kreditkarte, …*

1. Sort into matching pairs 1. d 2. c 3. e 4. b 5. a
2. Fill in the gaps Here there are several possibilities, the first one always being the most obvious. 1. gekommen – *gefahren* would be understood, but no-one says this. The verb that goes with *Flugzeug* (= plane) is *fliegen* (= to fly). The past participle is *geflogen,* but that's a bit complicated as yet. 2. gegeben – *gekauft* would also have been possible. 3. vergessen 4. gefahren / gekommen 5. angerufen / gebucht 6. gebucht / bezahlt 7. gearbeitet 8. bezahlt 9. gekauft / vergessen
3. Ask if there are any … here You can always look up the plural form in the dictionary at the back of the book. 1. Gibt es hier Taxis? 2. Gibt es hier Bücher? 3. Gibt es hier Briefmarken? 4. Gibt es hier Geschenke? 5. Gibt es hier Telefonkarten? 6. Gibt es hier Computer? 7. Gibt es hier Hotels? 8. Gibt es hier Banken?
4. What did you do when? 1. Ich bin vor drei Tagen nach München gefahren. 2. Ich habe vor fünf Minuten im Hotel angerufen. 3. Ich habe um elf ein Fax gesendet. 4. Ich habe vor vier Tagen ein schönes Buch gekauft. 5. Ich bin um vier Uhr ins Hotel gekommen. 6. Ich habe vor zehn Jahren in Wien gelebt. – Congratulations, this is an important step forward. It doesn't sound quite as convincing when you can speak only in the present tense. Now you can say quite a few things in the past.
5. Say how much it is 1. Die Fahrkarte kostet vierundfünfzig Mark. 2. Das Geschenk kostet neunzehn Mark. 3. Der Käse kostet vier Mark fünfzig. 4. Die Telefonkarte kostet zwölf Mark. 5. Das Weißbrot kostet drei Mark achtzig. 6. Die Zeitung kostet eine (!) Mark fünfzig. 7. Das Zimmer kostet neunzig Mark. 8. Die Wurst kostet sechs Mark zwanzig. 9. Die Postkarte kostet eine Mark zwanzig. – *Kostet* is the singular form of the verb. In the plural it is of course *kosten: Zwei Postkarten kosten zwei Mark vierzig.*

1. What's the plural? 1. die Personen 2. die Zimmer 3. die Taxis / Taxen – Many words that are not of German origin, in other words foreign words and modern international words take an -s in the plural. 4. die Brote 5. die Pässe 6. die Bücher 7. die Züge 8. die Hotels – See sentence 3. 9. die Schlüssel – Note that *Pass, Buch* and *Zug* have an umlaut in the plural: *Pässe, Bücher, Züge.*

2. The right answer 1. b – a is wrong, don't be confused because a word from the question also occurs in the answer. The return question about the time is justified because you can't always still get breakfast in a hotel at 10 o'clock. 2. b – a would be right if it was in the negative: *Nein, ich kann die Schlüssel nicht finden.* 3. a – *Zug* and *Taxi* are both means of transport, it's true, but in the context have little to do with one another, so b is wrong. 4. a – *buchen* simply means recording something in a book. It has nothing to do with a book you want to read, so a is right. 5. a – It's very nice when you go to pay and find someone else has already done it for you. If you've marked b, you've fallen into the same trap again. Take care with words that sound the same.

3. Say what you can't find The stumbling blocks are in sentences 1, 4, 5 7, 9 and 10, when *der* is changed to *den.* 1. Ich kann den Schlüssel nicht finden. 2. Ich kann das Buch nicht finden. 3. Ich kann die Zeitung nicht finden. 4. Ich kann den Computer nicht finden. 5. Ich kann den Rotwein nicht finden. 6. Ich kann die Fahrkarte nicht finden. 7. Ich kann den Käse nicht finden. 8. Ich kann das Ticket nicht finden. 9. Ich kann den Brief nicht finden. 10. Ich kann den Zug nicht finden.

4. Put them together The other possibilities are given in brackets. 1. d 2. e (c) 3. b 4. a 5. c (a, b, e) – The alternative answers don't always make a lot of sense, but they are grammatically correct.

1. Put in the right order 1. Das Flugzeug hat drei Stunden Verspätung. 2. Ich habe eine Reise gebucht. 3. Wir möchten nach Österreich in die Berge fahren. 4. Das Wetter ist heute keine Katastrophe. 5. Mein Zimmer ist schlecht und laut. – The word order in German is not simple and there are many possibilities. The general rule is that whatever is being given the main emphasis in a sentence comes right at the beginning. This cannot of course apply to the verb, which only comes at the beginning in a question. Other possible solutions: 1. Drei Stunden Verspätung hat das Flugzeug. 2. Eine Reise habe ich gebucht. 3. Nach Österreich in die Berge möchten wir fahren. 4. Keine Katastrophe ist das Wetter heute. 5. Schlecht und laut ist mein Zimmer.

2. Give your opinion 1. Ich finde, Urlaub ist schön. 2. Ich finde, das Hotel ist laut. 3. Ich finde, das Buch ist interessant. 4. Ich finde, die Zeitung ist schlecht. 5. Ich finde, der Computer ist gut. 6. Ich finde, die Idee ist wunderbar. 7. Ich finde, der Hotelmanager ist neugierig. 8. Ich finde, die Reise ist schön. 9. Ich finde, Urlaub ist besser als arbeiten. – The other possibility, which is just as common in both the written and spoken word, is a subordinate clause with *dass* (= that): *Ich finde, dass Urlaub schön ist. Ich finde, dass Urlaub besser als arbeiten ist.* Have patience, all will be explained in due course.

3. Read aloud 1. Das ist der zwölfte Stock, hier ist mein Zimmer. 2. Das ist der vierte Brief von Jürgen. 3. Nehmen Sie die dritte Straße links. 4. Der zweite Rotwein ist sehr gut. 5. Das ist die erste gute Idee. – When you've got *erste, zweite, dritte* and *siebte* into your head then you know the ordinal numbers, up to 20 with -te, from 20 on with -ste.

4. Sense or nonsense? Translate 1. Ich schulde Ihnen eine Idee. 2. Gibt es hier eine Bank mit Leben? 3. Wünschen Sie eine Wurst am Bahnhof? 4. Mein Computer hat Urlaub. 5. Eine Entschuldigung kostet nichts. – A grain of truth or at least a possible meaning can probably be found in every sentence.

5. Give your opinion again 1. Ich finde die Reise wunderbar. 2. Ich finde den Hotelmanager neugierig. 3. Ich finde die Idee schön. 4. Ich finde den Computer laut. 5. Ich finde die Zeitung interessant. 6. Ich finde das Buch schlecht. 7. Ich finde das Hotel gut. 8. Ich finde Urlaub schön. – Now you can say a lot. With these sentences, incidentally, you could write a nice little flirting dialogue. He says to her: *Ich finde Sie schön. Ich finde Sie interessant. Ich finde Sie wunderbar! Sind Sie verheiratet?* She to him: *Ich finde Sie neugierig!*

1. Which is right? 1. a 2. b 3. b 4. c 5. c 6. b
2. Answers and questions 1. c 2. f 3. e 4. d 5. b 6. a
3. Multiple choice 1. b 2. c 3. a 4. b 5. c 6. b
4. Sense and nonsense 1. Verspätung ist teuer. 2. Die Telefonkarte ist eine Katastrophe. 3. Ich brauche die Berge. 4. Nehmen Sie eine Katastrophe? 5. Geben Sie mir eine Fluglinie. 6. Das Wetter ist im 13. Stock.

1. Make a recommendation – Such sentences can be used to recommend practically anything that you might hand to someone. 1. Hier ist Käse. Der ist sehr gut. 2. Hier ist Vollkornbrot. Das ist gesund. 3. Hier ist Rotwein. Der ist wunderbar. 4. Hier ist Wurst. Die ist nicht schlecht. 5. Hier ist ein Buch. Das ist interessant. 6. Hier ist eine Postkarte. Die ist schön. 7. Hier ist eine Idee. Die ist sehr gut. – This example might sound a bit strange, but imagine the idea is written down on a piece of paper that you are handing to someone. 8. Hier ist eine Zeitung. Die ist nicht schlecht.

2. Ask a favour – *Mir* means "to me" in numbers 1, 3 , 5, and 6, and "for me" in 2, 4, 7 and 8. 1. Geben Sie mir bitte einen Kaffee. 2. Kaufen Sie mir bitte eine Fahrkarte. 3. Sagen Sie mir bitte Bescheid. 4. Machen Sie mir bitte eine Pizza. 5. Zahlen Sie (mir) bitte mit Kreditkarte. – Here you would leave the *mir* out. 6. Geben Sie mir bitte drei Briefmarken. 7. Finden Sie mir bitte das Hotel. 8. Buchen Sie mir bitte die Reise.

3. Find the partners 1. e – This is what you might say in the morning when greeting a guest. 2. c – Early in the morning. 3. a – When you want to relate some news. 4. d – When you want to make sure the other person doesn't give a wrong answer. 5. b – When you had your doubts beforehand and have been proved right.

4. Find the right answer 1. a – Both answers are appropriate in the morning. If someone calls *Frühstück ist fertig!*, however, they want the other person to come to the table, so the answer can't be b. 2. a – Here *es geht* means "not so well". 3. a – Coffee is for drinking, muesli for eating, so b can't be right. 4. a – *Natürlich* is a clear, reproachful *ja* when someone is reading the paper and doesn't want to be disturbed.

1. What's missing? 1. geschlafen 2. möchten 3. hätte 4. Bäcker – *Brot* is very important in Germany. *Vom Bäcker* means the bread has not come *aus dem Supermarkt* (= from the supermarket), so the quality is better. 5. Tasse – Some people are said to be addicted to coffee. For them one cup is not enough and it would be more appropriate to say: *Möchten Sie eine Kanne* (pot) *Kaffee?*
2. Gastronomic translation 1. coffee with milk 2. fruit with sugar 3. a pizza with cheese. 4. bread / sandwich with ham – In a café you would order a *Schinkenbrot:* an open ham sandwich. 5. muesli with yoghurt 6. tea with sugar 7. breakfast with juice 8. quark with jam – A *Pizza mit Käse* is not, incidentally, something you would normally get in a café. And certainly not for breakfast.
3. What would you like? 1. Ich hätte gerne eine schöne Küche. – What the wife says to the

husband. 2. Ich hätte gerne ein Ticket nach Wien. – What you say when you've had it up to here and want to go away. 3. Ich hätte gerne die Kreditkarte von Bill Clinton. – Not that the American President is very rich, but he's almost certainly not short of a dollar or two. 4. Ich hätte gerne keine Katastrophe mit meiner Frau. – Says the man who doesn't want to lose his wife. 5. Ich hätte gerne Reiseschecks in Rubel. – Says someone who has no idea what it's like in Russia. 6. Ich hätte gerne eine schöne Pizza. – Says a hungry man. 7. Ich hätte gerne ein Vier-Minuten-Ei. – Says someone for whom every detail of breakfast has to be right. 8. Ich hätte gerne einen roten Ferrari. – The favourite dream of many.

4. Put in the past tense – All the verbs are weak, i.e. the past participle has a *ge-* before the verb and the ending *-t*. Exception: *vergessen*. 1. Haben Sie das geglaubt? 2. Haben Sie die Frage vergessen? 3. Haben Sie gut geschlafen? 4. Haben Sie in Bern gelebt? 5. Haben Sie das gehört? 6. Haben Sie Bescheid gesagt?

5. Scrambled eggs 1. Ich komme ja schon. 2. Vollkornbrot ist sehr gesund. 3. Frühstück mit Müsli schmeckt gut. 4. Ich sage Bescheid in der Küche. 5. Ich hätte gerne ein Vier-Minuten-Ei. – As you know, the word order can be varied. The sentences could therefore also be constructed as follows: 1. Ja, ich komme schon. 4. In der Küche sage ich Bescheid. – This emphasizes *Küche,* perhaps as opposed to the living room or the street. 5. Ein Vier-Minuten-Ei hätte ich gerne.

14   Exercises A

1. Say it simply 1. Ich komme morgen mit. 2. Ich rufe Sie heute Abend an. 3. Ich checke bei Lufthansa ein. 4. Ich rufe Frau Krug jetzt zurück. 5. Ich fahre für drei Monate weg. – This by the way is one of the main difficulties in German: the verb, or parts of it, go to the end of the sentence. It's just something you have to get used to and keep repeating until it comes automatically.

2. Find the right translation 1. c 2. b – *fliegen mit dem Flugzeug* (= fly by plane) could also theoretically be said. 3. a 4. d

3. Which answer is right? 1. a – Although b would be possible, it would only be if the other person wants to ignore the suggestion. 2. b – a would only be possible in a context such as the following: *Ich brauche unbedingt eine Pizza. Ich habe nämlich Hunger. nämlich* has an explanatory function. 3. b – Actually it should be *Nein, lieber mit dem Taxi.* 4. a – This is what someone says who doesn't want the other person to pay.

4. Say no 1. Nein, ich möchte Ihnen nichts sagen. 2. Nein, ich möchte Ihnen nichts geben. 3. Nein, ich möchte Ihnen nichts raten. 4. Nein, ich möchte Ihnen nichts wünschen. 5. Nein, ich möchte Ihnen nichts zahlen. – There are cultures where it's impolite to say *nein.* This is not, however, the case in Germany.

14   Exercises B

1. Supply the accusative 1. mich 2. Sie 3. uns 4. mich 5. uns 6. Sie 7. mich 8. mich – A few more examples: *Rufen Sie mich an. Verstehen Sie mich? Brauchen Sie mich noch?*

2. Translate into English 1. I would like something to eat. 2. Let's rather go on foot. 3. The drinks first, please! 4. We're cooking in the kitchen. – Well, where else would you be doing that? 5. I would in fact (actually) like to eat. 6. We can take my car.

3. You are the waiter in an empty restaurant 1. Tut mir Leid, wir haben keine Getränke. 2. Tut mir Leid, wir haben keine Hamburger. 3. Tut mir Leid, wir haben keine Pizzas. 4. Tut mir Leid, wir haben keine Bratwürste. 5. Tut mir Leid, wir haben keinen Zucker. 6. Tut mir Leid, wir haben keinen Kaffee. 7. Tut mir Leid, wir haben keine Milch. 8. Tut mir Leid, wir haben keinen Tee. – A restaurant short of so many things should probably close...

4. Say what someone has done ... – This is a typical characteristic of German: in the perfect tense the verb (past participle) goes right to the end. People sometimes make fun of the word order, saying that in some German sentences you have to wait half an hour before the verb comes and you find out what it's all about. 1. Sie haben gut geschlafen. 2. Sie haben etwas zu essen gekocht. 3. Sie haben in der Küche Bescheid gesagt. 4. Sie haben die Frage nicht gehört. 5. Sie haben mich eingeladen. 6. Sie haben das Frühstück gezahlt.

5. Answers and questions – There are other possibilities aside from the official solution. 1. e 2. d (e) 3. c 4. a (e) 5. b (d, e)

1. Give the English for the following: 1. Mushroom allergy 2. Cheese sandwich 3. Bank card 4. Buttermilk 5. Milk soup (gruel) 6. Coffee cup 7. Ticket 8. Bread and butter sprinkled with sugar. – Do you know what *Zuckerbrot und Peitsche* (= whip) is? It's the equivalent of a stick and a carrot. 9. Holiday weather. – This always has to be good, woe betide if it rains! 10. Technical problem 11. Traveller's cheque 12. Room key 13. Journalist's wife. – This is not a female journalist, but the wife of a journalist. 14. Computer newspaper. – There are newspapers for everything: cars, travel, money or stamps.

2. You are the waiter in a five-star restaurant 1. Darf ich Ihnen noch einen Sherry bringen? 2. Darf ich Ihnen noch einen Rotwein bringen? 3. Darf ich Ihnen noch einen Sauerbraten bringen? 4. Darf ich Ihnen noch eine Käse-Pizza bringen? 5. Darf ich Ihnen noch eine Broccoli-Creme-Suppe mit Käse-Blätterteig bringen? 6. Darf ich Ihnen noch eine Bratwurst bringen? 7. Darf ich Ihnen noch eine Vorspeise bringen? 8. Darf ich Ihnen noch eine zweite Vorspeise bringen? 9. Darf ich Ihnen noch einen Kuchen bringen? – The other way of asking, which is not quite as polite, is *Möchten Sie noch einen Sherry?, einen Rotwein?* etc.

3. Questions and answers 1. a – *Vielleicht* always sounds polite, and the other person replies *lieber nicht* and agreement is reached... 2. a – b would be right if it was *Ich möchte nur Champignon-Suppe.* 3. a – Don't be confused by similar sounds. 4. b – Anyone who says a doesn't know what sherry is, or thinks it is a juice. Actually he's right, sherry is made from grapes.

4. Give the German translation 1. Nein, auf keinen Fall. – This is the most emphatic way of saying no. 2. Kommt sofort. – If you don't trust the waiter, ask *Wann sofort?* 3. Was möchten Sie als Vorspeise? 4. Ich habe eine Käse-Allergie. – Allergies can be used as an excuse for everything: *Ich habe eine Auto-Allergie, ich nehme das Flugzeug. Ich habe eine Coca-Cola-Allergie, ich trinke eine Pepsi.* 5. Können Sie mir eine Bratwurst bringen? – In the better restaurants you won't get a *Bratwurst,* which rates as a cheap meal or a snack between meals. 6. Tut mir Leid, ich habe das nicht. – It's frustrating when you find something really good on the menu and the restaurant's run out of it.

1. Put in the past tense 1. Ich war in Köln. – Now I'm here. 2. Hatten Sie schon Urlaub? – Or are you still going on holiday? 3. Wir waren neugierig. – Now we know everything and are no longer curious. 4. Waren Sie im Hotel? – Or did you stay with friends or sleep on the beach or under a bridge? 5. Herr Muller war Journalist. – Now he's doing something else. 6. Ich war verheiratet. – Now I'm divorced.

2. Which question is right? 1. a – The answer to b might for example be *Ja, kommt sofort.* 2. a – The answer to b might for example be Ja, bitte. 3. a – The answer to b might for example be *Zwei Sauerbraten und einen Salat.* 4. b – The answer to a might for example be *Ja, ich gebe immer Trinkgeld.* Or: *Nein, nie* (= No never).

3. Adding up the bill – If you have a restaurant in Germany and employ someone whose mother tongue is not German, give him this exercise to do. You will then see if he can add up and has enough German to take customers' money. 1. Zwei Wein – sieben Mark, ein Wasser – drei Mark, macht zusammen zehn Mark. 2. Eine Pizza – elf Mark, ein Bier – vier Mark zwanzig, macht zusammen fünfzehn Mark zwanzig. 3. Drei Käsebrot – achtzehn Mark, drei Wasser – sieben Mark fünfzig, macht zusammen fünfundzwanzig Mark fünfzig. 4. Zwei Bratwürste – neun Mark, eine Cola – drei Mark. Macht zusammen zwölf Mark. 5. Vier Hamburger – sechzehn Mark, ein Wein vier Mark fünfzig. Macht zusammen zwanzig Mark fünfzig. 6. Zwei Wasser – sechs Mark, eine Suppe sieben Mark. Macht zusammen dreizehn Mark. 7. Fünf Schinkenbrote – zweiunddreißig Mark fünfzig, fünf Cola – zwölf Mark. Macht zusammen vierundvierzig Mark fünfzig.

4. Put in the first person 1. Ich empfehle Sauerbraten. – Says the waiter, when he's asked for a recommendation, or when the braised beef in the kitchen is already five days old and really should be sold today... 2. Ich esse heute nichts. – Some people fully intend to do this in order to slim and are then confronted with a fridge full of food... 3. Ich bringe die Karte. 4. Ich zahle zwei Wein. 5. Ich komme sofort. 6. Ich gebe kein Trinkgeld. – That's not very nice when the waiter is friendly, but understandable when he's unfriendly.

1. Ask if you can do something 1. Soll ich Ihnen die 100 Dollars wechseln? – The bank has already closed and the other person needs money. 2. Soll ich Sie heute Abend anrufen? 3. Soll ich für Sie nach Berlin fahren? – And do something for the other person there. 4. Soll ich zu der Party mitkommen? 5. Soll ich mal raten? – I know, in fact, what's behind this. 6. Soll ich den Zug nehmen? 7. Soll ich das alles vergessen? – No, I don't want to forget it! 8. Soll ich den Sherry alleine trinken? – Come on, have a drink with me. 9. Soll ich das wirklich glauben? – No it's not true.

2. Find the right question 1. a – Possible answer to b: *Ja, gerne.* Or: *Nein, das geht leider nicht.* 2. a – Possible answer to b: *So gegen acht.* 3. b – Possible answer to a: *Natürlich.* Or: *Leider nicht. Bringen Sie doch bitte Champagner mit.* 4. b – Possible answer to a: *Ja, morgen. Möchten Sie kommen?*

3. Have a guess – People who like doing crosswords will have the least problems with this. 1. das Trinkgeld 2. der rheinische Sauerbraten 3. die Karte 4. die Party 5. neugierig

4. Sort into matching pairs 1. c 2. e 3. d 4. a 5. b – c and e would of course also fit here.

1. Put in the right order 1. Ich möchte Sie zu uns einladen. 2. Zuerst möchte ich aber etwas essen. 3. Es sind schon andere Gäste da. 4. Es kommen viele interessante Leute. 5. Es ist für alles gesorgt. – Other possibilities: 1. Zu uns möchte ich Sie einladen. Or: Sie möchte ich zu uns einladen. 2. Ich möchte aber zuerst etwas essen. 3. Andere Gäste sind schon da. – In this case the es is left out. 4. Viele interessante Leute kommen. – As in 3. 5. Für alles ist gesorgt. – As in 3 and 4.

2. What is it in English? 1. all day 2. to bring a present 3. around nine 4. I'm glad 5. other guests are already here 6. come in 7. that's not necessary 8. dance 9. take off your coat. 10. at the back in the kitchen.

3. Put these sentences in the plural – Actually it's easy in German with the singular and plural. There are languages which also have a dual form in the plural, in other words they distinguish between one, two and more than two. 1. Ich brauche die Pässe. 2. Wo sind (!) die Ausgänge? 3. Die Züge sind mir lieber. 4. Wir essen heute die Würste. 5. Die Gäste schlafen heute hier. – Have you noticed, *schlafen* is irregular, it's *er/sie schläft.* 6. Ich finde die Bücher interessant.

4. Sort into matching pairs – Here there's only one possibility. 1. d 2. e 3. a 4. f 5. c 6. b
5. What's missing? 1. ganzen 2. rein / mit 3. einladen 4. alles 5. mich

1. Which is right? 1. a 2. c 3. a 4. b 5. c 6. b
2. Answers and questions 1. e 2. f 3. a 4. b 5.c 6. d
3. Multiple choice 1. a 2. c 3. b 4. b 5. b 6. a
4. Sense and nonsense 1. Zahlen Sie mit Bratwurst? 2. Es sind schon andere Sauerbraten da. 3. Wir kochen morgen eine Party. 4. Ich habe schon den ganzen Tag Vorspeise. 5. Haben Sie eine Party-Allergie? 6. Ich möchte Sie vergessen.

1. Introduce someone 1. Darf ich Ihnen meine Frau vorstellen. 2. Darf ich Ihnen meinen Mann vorstellen? 3. Darf ich Ihnen meinen Freund Georg Jacobi vorstellen? 4. Darf ich Ihnen meine Freundin Claire Wilberg aus London vorstellen? 5. Darf ich Ihnen den Musiker Hans Werner Henze vorstellen? 6. Darf ich Ihnen den Ingenieur Dr. Jochen Hucke vorstellen? 7. Darf ich Ihnen meinen Professor vorstellen? 8. Darf ich Ihnen meine Freundin vorstellen? 9. Darf ich Ihnen den Filmschauspieler Dustin Hofmann vorstellen? – There is of course a less formal way of making introductions: *Meine Frau!* or: *Mein Mann!* or: *Dustin Hofmann.* But everyone knows him anyway.
2. Put them together 1. d 2. e – From a grammatical point of view c would also be possible, but a career as a film actor was not quite in Beethoven's line... Even had it been thought of then. 3. b 4. a 5. c – Götz George is such a good film actor that he would probably make a bad musician. So e is only possible from a grammatical point of view.
3. Find the right pronoun: mich, ihn, sie, Sie, uns? 1. ihn 2. Sie 3. uns 4. mich – The other way round hopefully too. 5. ihn 6. Sie 7. mich – This is what the end of a relationship might sound like. 8. sie – It may sound funny to have *sie* following *Sie,* but it often happens (and the other way round.) 9. uns
4. Fruit salad 1. Ich darf Ihnen einen interessanten Gast vorstellen. 2. Petra möchte uns eine Suppe kochen. 3. Maria findet mich sehr nett. 4. Ich finde sie auch besonders nett. 5. Darf ich Sie zu einem Wein einladen? – Other possibilities: 1. Ihnen darf ich einen interessanten Gast vorstellen. Or: Einen interessanten Gast darf ich Ihnen vorstellen. 2. Eine Suppe möchte Petra uns kochen. Or: Uns möchte Petra eine Suppe kochen. 3. Sehr nett findet Maria mich. Or: Mich findet Maria sehr nett. 4. Sie finde ich auch besonders nett. 5. Darf ich Sie zu einem Wein einladen? – Here there is no other alternative because it's a question and the verb always has to come at the beginning.

1. Have you got any dollars left? 1. Nein, ich habe keine Dollars mehr. 2. Nein, ich bekomme kein Bier mehr. 3. Nein, ich möchte keine Pizza mehr. 4. Nein, ich brauche keine Reiseschecks mehr. 5. Nein, ich habe keine Kreditkarte mehr. 6. Nein, ich schulde Ihnen kein Geld mehr. – This question has probably been put by someone who is very forgetful. Or unmaterialistic. 7. Nein, ich wünsche nichts mehr. 8. Nein, ich verstehe nichts mehr. – Or better: Nein, ich verstehe nicht mehr viel. 9. Nein, ich bringe morgen nichts mehr mit.
2. Give the German for the following... 1. der Bundeskanzler 2. der Bürgermeister 3. der Zuschauer 4. das Fernsehen 5. der Bundesfinanzminister 6. die Presse. – The German word for popular press is incidentally *Boulevard-Presse.*
3. Are you still working? 1. Nein, ich arbeite nicht mehr. 2. Nein, ich kaufe heute nicht mehr ein. 3. Nein, ich glaube das nicht mehr. 4. Nein, ich finde ihn nicht mehr nett.

5. Nein, ich zahle heute nicht mehr. 6. Nein, ich bleibe nicht mehr. 7. Nein, ich fahre nicht mehr nach München. 8. Nein, ich lebe nicht mehr. – Not a sentence to be taken too seriously.

4. Put in the past tense 1. Herr Carls ist heute nicht zurückgekommen. 2. Peter Urban ist nicht weggefahren. 3. Hans Meisner hat nicht angerufen. 4. Georg Biesalski hat uns eingeladen. 5. Ursula Steffens hat nicht zurückgerufen. 6. Wir sind weggefahren. 7. Marta Greisel hat eingekauft. 8. Theo Storch ist gerne mitgekommen. 9. Jürgen Frank hat sofort zurückgerufen. – The separable verbs are actually easier in the perfect tense, because they aren't separated any more but come in their complete form at the end of the sentence.

5. Fill in the gaps 1. Bundeskanzler 2. zurückgekommen 3. Presse 4. mitgeteilt 5. Filmschauspieler 6. Zuschauer

1. I don't like it/them either 1. Ich mag auch keine Filme. – That is something that few people would say. 2. Ich mag auch keine Zeitungen. 3. Ich mag auch keine Bratwurst. – Says the vegetarian fervently. 4. Ich mag auch kein Bier. 5. Ich mag auch keine Zuschauer. 6. Ich mag auch keine Bahnhöfe. – That's understandable, stations are always the scene of prolonged farewells. 7. Ich mag auch keinen Sauerbraten. 8. Ich mag auch keine Bundeskanzler. – Disinterest in politics is a sign of the times. 9. Ich mag auch keine Rechnungen. – Does anyone like paying? 10. Ich mag auch keine Verspätungen. – How about a bit more tolerance?

2. Which answer is right? 1. a – *Was möchten Sie frühstücken?* or *Kommen Sie doch zum Frühstück* would fit answer b. 2. b – A question to go with a could be *Tanzen Sie nicht gerne?* 3. a – A question to go with b could be *Mögen Sie keine Hotels* or *Reisen Sie nicht gerne?* 4. a – A question to go with b could be *Wer möchte noch etwas?* or *Wer hat noch eine Frage?* 5. a – A question to go with b could be *Haben Sie jetzt Zeit?*

3. The first approach – *Haben Sie Zeit* sometimes also means "Do you find me attractive?" 1. Haben Sie Zeit, darf ich Sie ins Kino einladen? 2. Haben Sie Zeit, darf ich Sie ins Theater einladen? 3. Haben Sie Zeit, darf ich Sie in die Disko einladen? 4. Haben Sie Zeit, darf ich Sie ins Restaurant einladen? 5. Haben Sie Zeit, darf ich Sie zum Frühstück einladen? 6. Haben Sie Zeit, darf ich Sie nach Acapulco einladen? 7. Haben Sie Zeit, darf ich Sie zu einer Party einladen? 8. Haben Sie Zeit, darf ich Sie ins Café einladen? 9. Haben Sie Zeit, darf ich Sie ins Hotel einladen? 10. Haben Sie Zeit, darf ich Sie zum Fernsehen einladen?

4. Form sentences – Here we don't need to imagine possible situations, because the second sentence after the comma always gives an explanation. 1. Ich mag keine Restaurants, ich esse nicht gerne. 2. Ich mag keine Telefone, ich rufe nicht gerne an 3. Ich mag keinen Rotwein, ich trinke nicht gerne. 4. Ich mag keine Probleme, ich rede nicht gerne. 5. Ich mag keine Parties, ich tanze nicht gerne. 6. Ich mag keinen Urlaub, ich reise nicht gerne. 7. Ich mag keine Supermärkte, ich kaufe nicht gerne ein. 8. Ich mag keine Diskos, ich tanze nicht gerne.

1. Form correct sentences 1. d 2. c or a 3. e 4. b 5. a or c

2. Translate into German 1. Ich tanze nicht gerne. 2. Ich habe keine Zeit. 3. Wir lassen uns scheiden. 4. Waren Sie beim Rechtsanwalt? 5. Wir haben uns getrennt. 6. Was hat er gesagt? 7. Darf ich Sie etwas fragen? 8. Meine Frau liebt einen anderen. – All these sentences sound like someone's going through a difficult time.

3. Put in the first person 1. Ich freue mich. 2. Ich trenne mich. 3. Ich lasse mich scheiden. 4. Ich sehe mich. – Sounds a bit strange, but what it might mean is in the mirror. 5. Ich vergesse mich. – This sentence could mean, I'm not myself today.

4. Say that something doesn't work – Every time you want to do something mad, someone comes along and says *Das können Sie nicht machen*. 1. Man kann sich doch nicht trennen, einfach so. 2. Man kann doch nicht im Restaurant tanzen, einfach so. 3. Man kann doch nicht beim Bundeskanzler anrufen, einfach so. 4. Man kann doch nicht Wasser essen, einfach so. 5. Man kann doch nicht im Urlaub arbeiten, einfach so. 6. Man kann doch nicht sieben Rotwein trinken, einfach so. 7. Man kann doch nicht zu Fuß nach Spanien gehen, einfach so. 8. Man kann doch nicht die Rechnung nicht bezahlen, einfach so. – Note: here *nicht* has to come twice.

1. Put it a different way 1. Mir tut der Kopf weh. 2. Mir tut der Bauch weh. 3. Mir tut der Rücken weh. 4. Mir tut der Fuß weh. 5. Mir tut die Welt weh. – This sentence is different, it's *die Welt*, whereas in all the other sentences the article is *der*. And something else is different: *Weltschmerz*, not *Weltschmerzen*.

2. Sort into matching pairs 1. c (a/b) – d would also be appropriate if it was *Nein, mir tut alles weh*. 2. d (a) 3. a 4. b (d)

3. Fill in the gaps 1. b 2. c – a would be right if it was *Sie müssen unbedingt gehen*. b is wrong because the article is already contained in *zum* (= zu dem) 3. b – The verb is *wehtun* and the *tun* is missing from the sentence.

4. Say what you must do 1. Ja, ich muss zum Arzt gehen. 2. Ja, ich muss morgen wegfahren. 3. Ja, ich muss heute arbeiten. 4. Ja, ich muss das Problem finden. – Here *Ja, ich finde das Problem* would be better, or *Nein, ich finde das Problem nicht.* 5. Ja, ich muss Geld wechseln. 6. Ja, ich muss unbedingt anrufen.

5. Asking for something at the chemist's – See also page 124, where the parts of the body are listed. 1. Ich brauche etwas gegen Rückenschmerzen. 2. Ich brauche etwas gegen Kopfschmerzen. 3. Ich brauche etwas gegen Fußschmerzen. 4. Ich brauche etwas gegen Bauchschmerzen. – Sometimes eating less might help. 5. Ich brauche etwas gegen Halsschmerzen. – Here not smoking might for example help.

1. *Wo fehlt's denn?* 1. Ich habe Fieber. 2. Ich habe Kopfschmerzen 3. Ich habe zu viel geraucht. 4. Ich habe gestern Abend getrunken. 5. Ich habe vielleicht einen Kater. 6. Ich habe Bauchschmerzen. – You can also say *Mir tut der Bauch weh.*

2. Put in the correct order 1. Alles tut mir weh. 2. Waren Sie schon einmal hier? 3. Ich habe gestern zu viel getrunken. 4. Haben Sie etwas Falsches gegessen? – Also possible: 1. Mir tut alles weh. 2. Waren Sie hier schon einmal? 3. Gestern habe ich zu viel getrunken. 4. Haben Sie etwas falsches gegessen? – With the question, the verb comes at the beginning so there is no alternative.

3. How does the sentence continue? 1. c 2. d 3. a 4. e 5. b – Here no alternatives are possible for reasons of grammar and content.

4. Put in the past tense 1. Ich habe vierzig Zigaretten geraucht. 2. Ich habe zwei Flaschen Kognak getrunken. 3. Ich habe drei Pizzas gegessen. 4. Ich habe 25 Stunden am Tag gearbeitet. 5. Ich habe Chinesisch gekocht. 6. Ich habe alles gesagt. – Weak verbs: *rauchen - geraucht, arbeiten - gearbeitet, kochen - gekocht, sagen - gesagt*. Strong verbs: *trinken - getrunken, essen - gegessen.*

5. Long words to translate 1. Braised beef 2. Olympic gold-medallist 3. Lawyers 4. Film actor 5. Cream of mushroom soup 6. Federal Minister of Finance – Common words like these are usually written without hyphens. But even on a menu you might well see *Champignon-Creme-Suppe*.

1. Put in the future tense 1. Ich werde in den Biergarten gehen. – Says someone who feels like some company. 2. Ich werde bestimmt wiederkommen. – Says someone who's going away. 3. Ich werde zum Bahnhof gehen. – This is also someone who's going away. 4. Ich werde meine Familie wieder sehen. – Says someone who's away. 5. Ich werde nach Zürich fahren. – Says someone who maybe wants to put a bit of spare cash in a reliable Swiss bank. 6. Ich werde zum Arzt gehen. – Says someone who's not feeling well and is perhaps ill. 7. Ich werde Kopfschmerzen haben. – Says someone confronted with an insurmountable problem. 8. Ich werde nicht mehr rauchen. – Says someone with smoke coming out of his ears. 9. Ich werde nie mehr trinken. – Says someone with a hangover. 10. Ich werde nicht sprechen. – Says someone who either wants to keep something a secret, or thinks the truth would be damaging, or simply wants to hold his tongue.

2. Find the right answer 1. a 2. a 3. b 4. a 5. a

3. Complete the sentence 1. c 2. d 3. b – d would also be right. 4. e 5. a

4. A family makes plans 1. Wir werden nach Österreich fahren. 2. Wir werden zusammen essen. 3. Wir werden den Freund vermissen. 4. Wir werden über alles reden. 5. Wir werden viel lachen. 6. Wir werden gut kochen und gut essen. 7. Wir werden im Supermarkt einkaufen. 8. Wir werden zusammen wegfahren.

1. Das gefällt mir – The verb *gefallen* can be used for any discussion involving likes and dislikes. 1. Der Film gefällt mir gut. 2. Das Buch gefällt mir nicht. 3. Die Filmschauspieler gefallen mir sehr. 4. Das Auto gefällt mir besonders. 5. Die Zeitungen gefallen mir nicht.

2. Translate into German 1. Wir werden dich vermissen. 2. Ich kann dich nicht vorher sehen. 3. Ich werde bestimmt wiederkommen. 4. Die Leute reden und rauchen. 5. Sie müssen jetzt zum Bahnhof. 6. Zehn Monate, das ist eine lange Zeit. 7. Warum fahren Sie nicht nach Deutschland?

3. Put in the first person 1. Ich lache viel. 2. Ich werde wiederkommen. 3. Ich spreche nicht. 4. Ich schreibe ein Buch. 5. Ich kann auch faxen. 6. Ich muss jetzt gehen. 7. Ich liebe.

4. You can say *du* to me 1. Du schreibst ein Buch. 2. Du kommst morgen wieder. 3. Du bringst das Geschenk. 4. Du trinkst Bier. 5. Du arbeitest viel. 6. Du lachst nie. – In the past it's *du hast getrunken, du bist gekommen, du hattest, du warst …* That will do for now.

1. Which is right? · 1. b 2. a 3. c 4. a 5. c 6. c

2. Answers and questions 1. e 2. a 3. d 4. c 5. b 6. f

3. Multiple choice 1. c 2. a 3. b 4. c 5. b 6. a

4. Sense and nonsense 1. Die Weinstuben und Biergärten lachen. 2. Der Bundesfinanzminister hat immer Kopfschmerzen. 3. Das Fieber und der Kater haben sich getrennt. 4. Ich vermisse meine Rückenschmerzen. 5. Der Papst und der Bundeskanzler rauchen im Kino. 6. Ich werde bestimmt den Rechtsanwalt wechseln.

Grammar summary

Regular conjugation

	arbeiten	to work		**machen**	to do
ich	arbeit-e	I work	ich	mach-e	I do
du	arbeit-est	you work	du	mach-st	you do
er/sie	arbeit-et	he/she works	er/sie	mach-t	he/she does
wir	arbeit-en	we work	wir	mach-en	we do
ihr	arbeit-et	you work	ihr	mach-t	you do
sie/Sie	arbeit-en	they/you work	sie/Sie	mache-n	they/you do

Also conjugated the same way:
brauchen, fragen, kommen, leben, lieben, rufen, sagen, senden, tanzen, zahlen etc.

Irregular conjugation

	schlafen	to sleep		**fahren**	to go
ich	schlaf-e	I sleep	ich	fahr-e	I go
du	schläf-st	you sleep	du	fähr-st	you go
er/sie	schläf-t	he/she sleeps	er/sie	fähr-t	he/she goes
wir	schlaf-en	we sleep	wir	fahr-en	we go
ihr	schlaf-t	you sleep	ihr	fahr-t	you go
sie/Sie	schlaf-en	they/you sleep	sie/Sie	fahre-n	they/you go

Also irregular:
einladen (du lädst ein) , fahren (du fährst), lassen (du lässt), nehmen (du nimmst), vergessen (du vergisst), wissen (du weisst)

Two very important verbs:

	sein	to be		**haben**	to have
ich	bin	I am	ich	hab-e	I have
du	bist	you are	du	ha-st	you have
er/sie	ist	he/she is	er/sie	ha-t	he/she has
wir	sind	we are	wir	hab-en	we have
ihr	seid	you are	ihr	hab-t	you have
sie/Sie	sind	they/you are	sie/Sie	hab-en	they/you have

Reflexive verbs

	sich freuen	to be glad
ich	freue mich	I am glad
du	freust dich	you are glad
er/sie	freut sich	he/she is glad
wir	freuen uns	we are glad
ihr	freut euch	you are glad
sie/Sie	freuen sich	they/you are glad

Also conjugated the same way: sich fragen, sich scheiden lassen (von), sich trennen (von), sich verstehen (mit + person)

Verbs   Past: The Perfect Tense

Ich **habe gearbeitet.**   I have worked.
Ich **bin** um sechs **gekommen.**   I came at six.

The perfect tense is constructed as follows:
1. the person *(ich)*
2. the appropriate form of *haben* or *sein (habe/bin)*
3. the past participle *(gearbeitet/gefahren)*

Usually the auxiliary verb is *haben,* but with verbs expressing motion it is *sein.*

The participle is usually formed as follows:
ge- + verb root + *-t/-et:*
kochen - ge-koch-t, leben - ge-leb-t, senden - ge-send-et etc.

Irregular verbs have irregular participles. The auxiliary verb used to form the perfect tense is given in brackets.

bekommen	bekommen (haben)	nehmen	genommen (haben)
bleiben	geblieben (sein)	rufen	gerufen (haben)
einladen	eingeladen (haben)	schlafen	geschlafen (haben)
essen	gegessen (haben)	sehen	gesehen (haben)
fahren	gefahren (sein)	sprechen	gesprochen (haben)
geben	gegeben (haben)	trinken	getrunken (haben)
gehen	gegangen (sein)	tun	getan (haben)
haben	gehabt (haben)	vergessen	vergessen (haben)
kommen	gekommen (sein)	wissen	gewusst (haben)

Verbs   Past: The Imperfect Tense

The imperfect is used a great deal in North Germany in both written and spoken German. The imperfect forms of *sein* and *haben* are used colloquially everywhere:

	sein			**haben**	
ich	war	I was	ich	hatt-e	I had
du	war-st	you were	du	hatt-est	you had
er/sie	war	he/she was	er/sie	hatt-e	he/she had
wir	war-en	we were	wir	hatt-en	we had
ihr	war-t	you were	ihr	hatt-et	you had
sie/Sie	war-en	they/you were	sie/Sie	hatt-en	they/you had

anrufen: Ich **rufe** Sie später **an.**   I'll call you later.
einladen: Frau Koch **hat** uns zu einer Party **eingeladen.**   Mrs Koch has invited us to a party.
wegfahren: Ich **fahre** morgen **weg.**   I am going away tomorrow.

When separable verbs are conjugated; the prefix goes to the end of the sentence.

Haben Sie schon **angerufen?**   Have you already called?
Er hat Sie **eingeladen.**   He has invited you.
Wir sind **weggefahren.**   We have gone away.

In the perfect, the participle of the separable verb goes to the end of the sentence. In the participle, -ge- is placed between the prefix and the verb.

anrufen	angerufen	vorstellen	vorgestellt
ausfüllen	ausgefüllt	wegfahren	weggefahren
einkaufen	eingekauft	wehtun	wehgetan
einladen	eingeladen	wiederkommen	wiedergekommen
einchecken	eingecheckt	zurückkommen	zurückgekommen
mitkommen	mitgekommen	zurückrufen	zurückgerufen
mitteilen	mitgeteilt		

Not to be confused with non-separable verbs with prefixes:

bekommen: Haben Sie den Brief bekommen?   Did you get the letter?
vergessen: Ich habe alles vergessen.   I have forgotten everything.

Mögen Sie noch einen Kaffee?   Would you like another coffee?
Darf ich Sie etwas fragen?   May I ask you something?
Ich **muss** morgen nach Hannover fahren.   I must go to Hanover tomorrow.
Soll ich noch einmal anrufen?   Should I call again?

Modal verbs are normally used with another verb in the infinitive.

	mögen			**dürfen**	
ich	mag	I like	ich	darf	I may
du	magst	you like	du	darfst	you may
er/sie	mag	he/she likes	er/sie	darf	he/she may
wir	mögen	we like	wir	dürfen	we may
ihr	mögt	you like	ihr	dürft	you may
sie/Sie	mögen	they/you like	sie/Sie	dürfen	they/you may
	müssen			**sollen**	
ich	muss	I must	ich	soll	I should
du	musst	you must	du	sollst	you should
er/sie	muss	he/she must	er/sie	soll	he/she should
wir	müssen	we must	wir	sollen	we should
ihr	müsst	you must	ihr	sollt	you should
sie/Sie	müssen	they/you must	sie/Sie	sollen	they/you should

können

ich	kann	I can
du	kannst	you can
er/sie	kann	he/she can
wir	können	we can
ihr	könnt	you can
sie/Sie	können	they/you can

Verbs — The Future

Ich **werde** morgen **anrufen.**   I'll call tomorrow

The future is a simple construction consisting of the appropriate form of *werden* + the verb in the infinitive.

ich	werde kommen	I will come
du	wirst kommen	you will come
er/sie	wird gehen	he/she will go
wir	werden trinken	we will drink
ihr	werdet kommen	you will come
sie/Sie	werden essen	they/you will eat

Articles — The Definite Article der/die/das

	singular	plural
masculine	**der** Bahnhof	**die** Bahnhöfe
feminine	**die** Zeitung	**die** Zeitungen
neuter	**das** Problem	**die** Probleme

Articles — The Indefinite Article ein/eine/ein

	singular	plural
masculine	**ein** Zug	Züge
feminine	**eine** Reise	Reisen
neuter	**ein** Problem	Probleme

Many verbs take the accusative, e.g. *Ich habe eine Frage.*

The masculine form of both articles changes in the accusative:

Articles — Accusative of the Definite Article

masculine	**den** Bahnhof	**die** Bahnhöfe
feminine	**die** Zeitung	**die** Zeitungen
neuter	**das** Problem	**die** Probleme

Articles — Accusative of the Indefinite Article

masculine	**einen** Bahnhof	Bahnhöfe
feminine	**eine** Zeitung	Zeitungen
neuter	**ein** Problem	Probleme

The plural of the definite article is *die* for all three forms (masculine, feminine, neuter). There is no indefinite article in the plural.

Nouns are like articles and pronouns:

masculine	feminine	neuter
der Film	die Butter	das Auto
der Name	die Straße	das Fernsehen
der Mann	die Frau	das Kind

1. like the singular: der Bäcker – die Bäcker, das Theater – die Theater
2. singular + -e: der Kurs – die Kurse, das Problem – die Probleme
3. singular + -n: die Dame – die Damen, der Name – die Namen
4. singular + -en: die Person – die Personen, die Frau – die Frauen
5. singular + -er: das Trinkgeld – die Trinkgelder,
6. singular + -s: das Café – die Cafés, das Taxi – die Taxis

der Zug	die Züge
der Mann	die Männer
die Wurst	die Würste
das Buch	die Bücher
der Kopf	die Köpfe
der Fuß	die Füße

These are formed by joining two nouns together:

Singular	Plural
der Haus-Schlüssel	die Haus-Schlüssel
die Platz-Reservierung	Platz-Reservierungen
das Kurs-Buch	die Kurs-Bücher

Note: the article (der/die/das) is always taken from the last noun in the compound.

Nominative		Accusative		Dative	
ich	I	mich	me	mir	to me
du	you	dich	you	dir	to you
er	he	ihn	him	ihm	to him
sie	she	sie	her	ihr	to her
es	it	es	it	ihm	to it
wir	we	uns	us	uns	to us
ihr	you	euch	you	euch	to you
Sie	you	Sie	you	Ihnen	to you
sie	they	sie	them	ihnen	to them

Pronouns — Possessive Adjectives

Pronouns		Possessive Adjectives	
ich	I	mein	my
du	you	dein	your
er	he	sein	his
sie	she	ihr	her
es	it	sein	its
wir	we	unser	our
ihr	you	euer	your
Sie	you	Ihr	your
sie	they	ihr	their

Prepositions

am Bahnhof	at the station
aus Frankreich	from France
bis morgen	until/by tomorrow
für Sie	for you
in Deutschland	in Germany
mit Bad	with bath
nach München	to Munich
ohne mich	without me
zu uns	to us

Certain prepositions are combined with certain articles: e.g.:

an de**m** Bahnhof	→ **am** Bahnhof
zu de**m** Hotel	→ **zum** Hotel
in de**m** Zimmer	→ **im** Zimmer
zu de**r** Zeitung	→ **zur** Zeitung
in da**s** Zimmer	→ **ins** Zimmer

Adverbs — Adverbs of Place

Adverbs	Adverbs of Place
dort	there
drüben	over there
hier	here
hinten	at the back
links	(on the) left
rechts	(on the) right
überall	everywhere

Adverbs — Adverbs of Time

Adverbs	Adverbs of Time
heute	today
jetzt	now
manchmal	sometimes
morgen	tomorrow
schon	already
sofort	right away
vorher	before(hand)
zuerst	first

alleine	alone
am besten	best
am meisten	most
besonders	particularly
besser	better
einfach	easily
falsch	wrongly
gut	well
in bar	in cash
nämlich	actually
natürlich	of course
noch	still
zu Fuß	on foot

Question words

was	what?	**Was** haben Sie gesagt?	What did you say?
wer	who?	**Wer** kommt morgen?	Who is coming tomorrow?
wo	where?	**Wo** ist das Hotel Atlantis, bitte?	Where is the Atlantis Hotel, please?
wann	when?	**Wann** sehen wir uns?	When are we going to see each other?
wie	how?	**Wie** geht es Ihnen?	How are you?
warum	why?	**Warum** fragen Sie nicht?	Why don't you ask?
welch	which?	**Welcher** Zug fährt nach Hof?	Which train goes to Hof?

Compound interrogatives:

wozu	to what?	wofür	for what?	womit	with what?

Numbers

1 eins	11 elf	21 einundzwanzig
2 zwei	12 zwölf	22 zweiundzwanzig
3 drei	13 dreizehn	23 dreiundzwanzig
4 vier	14 vierzehn	24 vierundzwanzig
5 fünf	15 fünfzehn	25 fünfundzwanzig
6 sechs	16 sechzehn	26 sechsundzwanzig
7 sieben	17 siebzehn	27 siebenundzwanzig
8 acht	18 achtzehn	28 achtundzwanzig
9 neun	19 neunzehn	29 neunundzwanzig
10 zehn	20 zwanzig	30 dreißig
		31 einunddreißig

40 vierzig	100 hundert
50 fünfzig	1000 tausend
60 sechzig	10.000 zehntausend
70 siebzig	100.000 hunderttausend
80 achtzig	1.000.000 eine Million
90 neunzig	1.000.000.000 eine Milliarde
	1.000.000.000.000 eine Billion

Numbers — Ordinal Numbers

1.	erste	first
2.	zwei-te	second
3.	dritte	third
4.	vier-te	fourth
5.	fünf-te	fifth
6.	sechs-te	sixth
7.	sieb-te	seventh
8.	ach-te	eighth
9.	neun-te	ninth
10.	zehn-te	tenth

Numbers — Time

1 sec	die Sekunde	second
60 sec	die Minute	minute
60 min	die Stunde	hour
24 h	der Tag	day
7 Tage	die Woche	week
4 Wochen + 2-3 Tage	der Monat	month
12 Monate / 356 Tage	das Jahr	year

Numbers — Clock Time

10.30 h	zehn Uhr dreißig
21.10 h	einundzwanzig Uhr zehn
um eins	at one (o'clock)
um zehn	at ten (o'clock)

um (= at) indicates the exact time.

Numbers — Arithmetic

$12 + 4 = 16$	zwölf **und** vier **sind** sechzehn
$15 - 4 = 11$	fünfzehn **weniger** vier **sind** elf
$5 \times 6 = 30$	fünf **mal** sechs **sind** dreißig
$21 / 7 = 3$	einundzwanzig **durch** sieben **sind** drei

+: *und* or *plus*   −: *weniger* or *minus*   x: *mal*

/: *durch* or *geteilt durch*   =: *sind* or *gleich*

Sentence Construction — Statements

Sie kommen morgen.	They come tomorrow.
Wir glauben das.	We believe that.

1. First comes the person or subject i.e. whatever is doing something.
2. Then comes the verb, i.e. the activity, what is happening.
3. Then the rest, objects *(wen, wem)*, adverbs *(wann, wie, wo)* etc.

Kommen Sie morgen?   Are you coming tomorrow.
Glauben wir das?   Do we believe that?

1. First comes the verb.
2. Then comes the person or the subject.
3. Then comes the rest.

Kommen Sie morgen!   Come tomorrow!
Glauben Sie das!   Believe that!

1. First comes the verb.
2. Then comes the person or the subject.
3. Then comes the rest.

In a statement the verb must always come second. Another part of the sentence can come first instead of the subject, which then goes to third place:

Wir fahren morgen mit dem Zug nach Hamburg.
We are going by train to Hamburg tomorrow.

Other possibilities:

Morgen	fahren	wir mit dem Zug nach Hamburg.
Mit dem Zug	fahren	wir morgen nach Hamburg.
Nach Hamburg	fahren	wir morgen mit dem Zug.

Capital letters are used at the beginning of a sentence, for all nouns and names, and for the polite forms of address *Sie, Ihnen* and *Ihr.*

Dictionary

Nouns are given with the relevant article *(der, die, das)* and with their plural form.
- means that the plural is the same as the singular; *-e, -en, -s* etc. means that this is added to the singular, and when the plural is completely different it is written out in full.
Separable verbs are written as follows: prefix | verb. Words beginning with *ge-* should be looked for without the *ge-*, i.e. you will find *gemacht* under *machen*.
The number indicates the page where the word in question first occurs.

A

ab	from ... on	67
ab|legen (abgelegen)	to take off (coat)	107
aber	but	27
acht	eight	35
achtzehn	eighteen	41
Alkoholiker, *der;* -	alcoholic	131
alleine	alone	29
Allergie, *die;* -n	allergy	99
alles	everything	15
als	as	99
am	at the	21
am besten	best	43
am meisten	most	131
an|rufen (angerufen)	to call, to phone	35
andere	other	55
arbeiten	to work	21
auch nicht	not ... either	23
auf	at, on	43
auf keinen Fall	on no account	99
auf Wiedersehen	goodbye	131
aus	from	11
aus|füllen	fill in	127
Ausgang, *der;* Ausgänge	exit	69
Auto, *das;* -s	car	93

B

Bäcker	baker	89
Bahnhof, *der;* Bahnhöfe	station	61
Bank, *die;* -en	bank	53
Bauch, *der;* Bäuche	stomach	125
Bauchschmerzen, *die* (Plural)	stomach-ache	125
bei uns	at our place/house	107
Beispiel, *das;* -e	example	81
bekommen (bekommen)	to get	41
Berg, *der;* -e	mountain	79
Bescheid sagen	to tell (sb)	89
besonders	particularly	113
besser als	better than	81
bestimmt	definitely	131
Biergarten, *der;* -gärten	beer garden	131
bin	am	9
bis	to	75
bitte	please	9
Blätterteig, *der*	pastry	99
bleiben (geblieben)	to stay	63

Bratwurst, *die;* Bratwürste	(fried) sausage	95
brauchen	to need	35
Brief, *der;* -e	letter	41
Briefmarke, *die;* -n	stamp	41
bringen (gebracht)	to bring	99
Broccoli, *der*	broccoli	99
Brot, *das;* -e	loaf/bread	47
Buch, *das;* Bücher	book	43
buchen	to reserve, book	75
Buchhandlung, *die;* -en	bookshop	43
Bundesfinanzminister, *der;* -	(Federal) Minister of Finance	115
Bundeskanzler, *der;* -	(Federal) Chancellor	115
Bürgermeister, *der;* -	mayor	115
Butter, *die*	butter	47

C

Café, *das;* -s	café	93
Champignon, *der;* -s	mushroom	99
Cola, *die;* -s	coke	95
Computer, *der;* -	computer	21
Creme, *die;* -n	cream	99

D

D-Mark, *die;* -	German mark	53
Dame, *die;* -n	lady	115
danke	thank you	15
Danke schön	thank you very much	37
dann	then	61
darf (gedurft)	may/can	49
das	that	9
das macht ...	that's	41
dass	that	115
der	the	41
Deutschland	Germany	131
dich	you	133
die	the	33
dir	to you	133
direkt	straight, direct	69
Disko, *die*	disco	119
doch bitte	do please	107
dort drüben	over there	73
drei	three	35
dreizehn	thirteen	41
dürfen (gedurft)	to be allowed to (do sth)	49

E

Ei, *das;* -er	egg	89
eigentlich schon	... in fact	121
ein bisschen	a bit	17
ein|checken	to check in	69
ein|kaufen	to go shopping, to buy	53
ein|laden (eingeladen)	to invite	93
einfach	easy	61
schon einmal	before, already	127
eins	one	35
elf	eleven	41
empfehlen (empfohlen)	to recommend	99
England	England	79
Entschuldigung, *die;* -en	excuse me	9
er	he	37
es gibt (es gab)	there is/are	73
es ist aus	it's all over	121
es ist was los	there's something going on	131
essen (gegessen)	to eat	95
etwas	something	93

F

fahren (gefahren)	to go, to travel	67
Fahrkarte, *die;* -n	ticket	67
falsch	wrong	127
Familie, *die;* -n	family	131
Fax, *das;* -e	fax	43
faxen	to fax	133
Fernsehen, *das*	television	113
fertig	ready	87
Fieber, *das*	temperature	127
Film, *der;* -e	film	119
Filmschauspieler, *der;* -	film actor	113
finden (gefunden)	to find	75
Fluglinie, *die;* -n	airline	69
Flugzeug, *das;* -e	plane	81
Formular, *das;* -e	form	127
Fotograf, *der;* -en	photographer	21
Frage, *die;* -n	question	27
fragen	to ask	119
Frau, *die;* -en	Ms, Mrs, Miss, woman	9
freuen, sich	to be glad	105
Freundin, *die;* -nen	(girl-)friend	29
Frühstück, *das*	breakfast	75